WEATHER
REPORTS

WEATHER REPORTS

NEW AND SELECTED POEMS BY QUINCY TROUPE

HARLEM RIVER PRESS
New York • London

Published for **HARLEM RIVER PRESS** by:
WRITERS AND READERS PUBLISHING, INC.
P.O.BOX 461, Village Station,
New York, New York 10014

Some of the poems in this volume were published in
the following magazines, to whom the author gives
grateful acknowledgement:
*Chicago International, Another Chicago Magazine,
Pequod, New Directions 22, Vox, New York Quarterly,
Ploughsharer, Sumac, Black Scholar, Umbra, Essence, The
Mediterranean Review, Encore, Black World, Yardbird,
Long Shot, Black Creation, Mundus Artium, Antioch
Review, River Styx 4, 5, 10, 12, Confrontation, Okike,
Nommo, Lotus, Nimrod, Poets & Writers, Indigine,
lacanian ink, Callaloo, Black Review, Contact II, World
Order, Conch, World 37, World 38, Helen Review, Crisis,
Drum, Quilt, Hard Pressed #7, Bopp, The Western
Journal of Black Thought, Iowa Review, The Village Voice,*
and *Ikon.*
Some of the poems were recorded on the audio tape
Shaman Man, by Quincy Troupe, released by the
Watershed Foundation, 1991.
ISBN 0-86316-108-1 Hardcover
ISBN 0-86316-003-4 Paperback

0 9 8 7 6 5 4 3 2 1

WEATHER REPORTS

TABLE OF CONTENTS

"Blues Laced Tongues"
The Poetry of Quincy Troupe

A generation of students and scholars of African-American literature and culture, growing up during the Sixties, a turbulent decade of socio-political and economic upheaval, was most familiar with resonance of the strident voices of such political giants as Malcolm X and Dr. Martin Luther King, Jr. But they also heard the cacophonous voices of such cultural giants as LeRoi Jones (Imamu Baraka), Don L. Lee (Haki Madhubuti), Nikki Giovanni, and Sonia Sanchez, who were the architects of a "Black Arts Movement." Describing it as the "æsthetic sister" of the Black Power Movement, Larry Neal argued justifyingly that, because there were "in fact and spirit two Americas—one black, one white," the Black artist had made the "spiritual and cultural needs of Black people" his primary duty.[1]

Among the voices of the rank and file of this group was St. Louis born poet Quincy Troupe, who, standing in the vanguard of the Watts Writers Workshop, was determined from the outset not only to meet the prescriptions of the Black Arts Movement, but perhaps more important to do so by indelibly impacting it through his work. This collection, *Weather Reports*, reveals that a commitment to the spiritual and cultural needs of Black people remains firmly intact for this award-winning journalist, essayist, novelist, poet, educator, editor, biographer and producer, who is currently Professor of Creative Writing at the University of California at San Diego.

Troupe's most impressive list of publications, including such original collections as *Embryo* (1972), *Snake-Back Solos* (1979), which won the American Book Award for poetry in 1980; and *Skulls Along the River* (1984), offers a clear measurement of both his progress and success. He has also edited *Giant Talk: An Anthology of Third World Writing* (1975) and *James Baldwin: The Legacy* (1989). His definitive

---

[1] Larry Neal, "The Black Arts Movement," in *The Black Æsthetics*, ed., Addison Gayle.

Miles: The Autobiography, Miles Davis with Quincy Troupe (1989) won the 1990 American Book Award.

In 1989, Troupe was featured on Bill Moyers' Emmy Award-winning series *"The Power of the Word."* This seems most appropriate, for it is the power of a language that is above all alive, communal, and musical which screams, dances, or whispers gently from Troupe's poetry and prose. "Language *is* life," he told Moyers, who equated the experiencing of Troupe's words and language to having a rocket race through one's brain.

For Troupe, language is culturally specific. It "comes from out of a place." "You must write from where you come from," he admonished a group of students at his alma mater, Beaumont High School in St. Louis. Thus, not surprisingly, his language not only speaks to an environment fashioned and affected by the meat packing houses of St. Louis ("Growing Up in River Rhythm") and the urban plight of Manhattan where he lived and worked for almost two decades ("Eighth Avenue Poem, Uptown" and "New York Bag Lady"), but also the cultural and spiritual needs of Black people everywhere—from Africa to America and the Caribbean islands—that he calls home. In his works he attempts to capture these places, sealing their blackness in the reverberating sounds of "black holes" that he, as artist-creator-poet-speaker, "sews" into his words, while celebrating a cultural specificity that illuminates a new truth.

In what is obviously a very personal voice, he declares through one of his speakers:

> my poems have holes sewn into them
> & they run, searching for light
> at the end of tunnels, they become trains
> or the bottom of pits, they become blackness
> or in the broad, winging daylight
> they are words that fly

> my poems have hole sewn into them
> & their voices are like different keyholes
> through which dumb men search for speech, blind
> men search for sight

> words, like drills, penetrating sleep
> keys unlocking keyholes of language
> words giving sight to blind peoples eyes . . .

In this language, which moves as rapidly as the beak and wings of a hummingbird, one finds the poet drawing, stitching and weaving images, words and sounds to (re)create, (re)define etymology, epistemology, astronomy, genealogy, and cosmology. His "black holes" are signifiers of, while signifyin(g) on, the slave ship's hold/hole described by Olaudah Equiano in his *Interesting Narrative* and experienced by millions of Africans who, as reluctant voyagers of a slave trade, journeyed, like collapsing stars, through the Middle Passage to a life of catastrophe in the "New World." Simultaneously, however, they are signifiers of, while signifyin(g) on the (w)hole-ness sought by Frederick Douglass and his fellow bondsmen and women in their quest for meaning and self.

More importantly, Troupe's "black holes" seek to recreate and validate the (w)hole-ness and communality of the nation of dancers, musicians, and poets of Equiano's African traditional world, whose density and complexity were grounded firmly in family and language: a key "to unlock keyholes," a light that "gives sight to the blind." It is this world—this supermassive black(w)hole/hold/hole— that remains lost in time and space, in a gravitational force of memory: the "hieroglyphics of space and time, forming/sculpting in the winds, from great distances, voice,/ shapes down way, way low," that attracts the poet. Continuously pulling him in are the now faceless "skulls along the river" that float in this imaginary one-way membrane of memory which he attempts to infuse with new life and meaning.

This idea is clearly echoed by the speaker of "The Old People Speak of Death":

> eye walk back now, with this poem
> through turnstile-holes the old folks left in their eyes
> for me to pass through, walk back to where eye see
> them there
> the ones who have gone beyond hardness

the ones who have gone beyond form
see them there
darker than where roots began
& lighter than where they go
carrying their spirits
heavier than stone, their memories
sometimes brighter than the flash
of sudden lightning.

Death is a rite of passage that results in aggregation with ancestors for the poet who now sees with a new "I/eye."

Unlike the stellar black hole which, for the most part, looses all information about the star that formed it, Troupe's "black hole" is saturated with the properties and qualities of the language that gives it form, in particular those found in the matrix of the blues and jazz vernacular; that is, in the colloquial falling from the "blues laced tongues" of a "blues people/ doing blues, dues thangs." A speaker prayerfully invokes:

grant me sacred light of your blues
doowopping mackmen
            grant me holyflight of your eagle-
winged life, grant me holy flight
of your eagle-winged life
o grant me the tongue, living
your blues, perfect eardrums.

With wish granted, the poet-speaker-singer's first person narrative voice, "I," transcends to a luminous and mediumistic "eye" that glides assessingly across generations of experiences, from collective and destructive slavery to the painful, the tragic life of Big Tom, the packing houseman who killed for pay, the Eighth Avenue junkies who have "shot so much shit/ into the soles of their feet," to the exhilarating choreographic moves of Magic Johnson, a quicksilver who wipes "glass backboards so clean."

Ultimately, *Weather Reports* reveals the degree to which Quincy Troupe has labored in the vineyard of his craft, not merely perfecting the prescriptions of the Black Arts Movement but perhaps best signifyin(g) its evolution as we move towards the Twenty-First Century. Through the autobiographical voice of the speaker in "Boomerang" he confesses:

> eye use to write poems about burning
> down the motherfucking country for crazy
> horse, geronimo & malcolm king
> x marks the spot where "coons" signed away
> their lives on dotted lines, black holes
> sucking away their breath . . .

The gravitational "black holes" in *Weather Reports* are thermometers and barometers of an "I"/"eye" that sees with expansive eyes and speaks with a deeper voice of the spiritual needs and achievements of Black people. These "black holes" open "spaces between worlds" and are simultaneously multifaceted "worlds themselves/words falling off into one another." Here one finds a different kind of journey, insights into the hieroglyphics of Black culture deeply encoded in the matrix of its language and the blues dues sounds of its songs. Troupe proves that he, too, like Magic, is a "sho-nuff spaceman" and shaman.

Wilfred D. Samuels, Ph.D.
Associate Professor of English
Director of Black Studies
University of Utah
Summer 1991

For Margaret

My Poems Have Holes Sewn In to Them

my poems have holes sewn into them
& they run, searching for light
at the end of tunnels, they become trains
or at the bottom of pits, they become blackness
or in the broad, winging daylight
they are words that fly

& holes are these words
letters, or syllables with feathered wings
that leave their marks on white pages
then, fly off, like footprints tracked in snow
& only God knows where they go

this poem has holes stitched into it
as our speech, which created poetry in the first place
lacerated, wounded words, that strike out original
meaning, bleeding into language
hemorrhaging, out of thick, or thin mouths
has empty spaces & silences sewn into it

my poems have holes sewn into them
& their voices are like different keyholes
through which dumb men search for speech, blind
men search for sight
words, like drills, penetrating sleep
keys unlocking keyholes of language
words giving sight to blind peoples eyes

my poems have holes sewn into them
& they are spaces between worlds
are worlds themselves
words falling off into one another

colliding, like people gone mad, they space out
fall, into bottomless pits, which are black
holes of letters that become words
& worlds, like silent space
between chords of a piano

they fall back, into themselves
into time, sleep
        bottom out, on the far side of consciousness
where words of all the worlds poets go
& whisper, in absolute silence

this poem has deep holes stitched into it
& their meanings have the deadly suck of quicksand
the irreversible pull of earth to any & all skydivers
the tortured pus-holes tracking arms of junkies

my poems have holes sewn into them
& they run, searching for light, at the end
of tunnels, or at the bottom of yawning pits
or in the broad daylight, where
the words, flapping like wings of birds
fly, whispering, in absolute silence

Embryo (1972)

White Weekend
April 5th to the 9th, 1968

they deployed military troops
surrounded the White House
& on the steps of the senate building
a soldier, behind a machine gun

32,000 in washington & chicago
1900 in baltimore maryland
76 cities in flames on the landscape
& the bearer of peace
lying still in atlanta

lamentations, lamentations, lamentations
worldwide
but in new york, on wall street
the stock market went up 18 points . . .

woke up crying the blues
bore witness to the sadness of the day
the peaceful man from atlanta
was slaughtered yesterday
got myself together
drank in the sweetness of sunshine
wrote three poems to the peaceful lamb
from atlanta, made love to a raging black woman
drank wine, the grapes of poets
got high, saw angels
leading the lamb to heaven? —
the blues gonna get me, gonna get me
for sure, went to the beach too
forget, if only eye can about the gentle
soul from georgia, ate
clam chowder soup & fish sandwiches
made love in the sand to this same
beautiful woman
drank in all her sweet —
ness, lost future child in the sand
saw a bloody sun falling behind
weeping, purple clouds
as tears fell in a cloudburst of warm rain
for this dreaming lamb eye cant forget
the bloody moon-star, sinking
into the purple, cloud tossed grave
blackness falls through praying
hours of day, go out into
the decay of sunlight
copped three keys —
the key of creative joy
the key of happiness

the key of subliminal sadness —
came back on a whim to her house
which was disrupted, watched the gloom
on the idiot tube, kissed her in a panic
then spaced all the way home
by route of the mad
deathway, dropped tears in my lap
for the turning cheek from atlanta
come home safe at last —
two letters under the door
grips at the root of my being—
a love letter from the past shakes up
whatever is left of that memory
at last another poem published
good news during a bad news weekend—
lights out, drink of grapes
severed sight closes
another day in the life

The Syntax of the Mind Grips

the syntax of the mind grips
the geography of letters
burns the symbols black, then leaves
the black ocean of oysters bleeds pearls
washes the shore where darkness crawls in
alone, like a panther, all luminous
eyes, watching us make love
under trees, the beautiful
woman in the grass
curls her pulling
legs around my shoulders
the old maid weeps in the window
covers her face with her blue veined, white hands
her fingernails painted red, gouges out her love
shattered eyes, as the mirror
breaks in the bathroom
falls like razor blades, glittering
on the floor, where a junkie is sprawled
a death needle in his arm, a child cuts his feet
in the streets, screams for the old maid who makes
the flags, weeping in the halloween window
because stars have fallen from the flags
she does not hear anything
inside her own weeping
because the flag has become a garrote
choking, the breath love from a people
whose hero is the armless, legless
brain dead vegetable
who sits upon his bandaged stump
in a wheelchair, in a veteran's hospital
in washington, they are giving him medals
he cannot speak-tell of the blood

he has swallowed
cannot see for the death
his eyes have seen, cannot hear
the screams his ears have heard
he feels the sorrow of the old maid
who is weeping because the stars have fallen
through the black holes of the torn flag
who is weeping because of the love
scene in wet grass beneath her window

Weather Report In Lincoln Nebraska 2/8/71
"It is the coldest night in 23 years in Lincoln Nebraska"
from a news report

outside my see-through mirror
snow was piled in frozen sculpture
grotesque along the bleak streets
of lincoln nebraska
while on television, apollo 14
streaked through unconquered space
after photographing holes
& collecting wierd rocks on a moon
that did not welcome them, also on this day
america was invading laos disguised
as south vietnamese troops — they recruited
a lot of slant eyed american dwarfs & hired
america's best makeup men to pull off
this standard american hat-trick

& in lincoln nebraska, the temperature
was twenty-five degrees below zero
but it was colder than that
within the pentagon ruled, executive tombs
in washington, it was so cold that nobody
as yet has recorded the temperature
& this suited tricky dick
just fine, sublime
he walked around naked
took a whirlpool bath
in a tub filled with laoian blood
while his handmade, good old
melvin, scrubbed his brain clean
with a redwhite & blue soapbar
of pure nitroglycerin

Chicago
For Howlin Wolf ▬▬▬▬▬▬▬▬▬▬▬▬▬▬▬▬▬▬▬▬▬▬▬▬▬▬▬

1.

the wind blade cuttin in
& out, swinging in over the lake
slicing white foam from the tips
of delicate water fingers
dancing & weaving
under the sunken light, night
& this wind blade was so sharp & cold
it'd cut a pole-legged mosquito into fours
while a hungry child slept down wind from some chittlins
slept within the cold blues of a poem that was formin
& we came in the sulphuric night drinkin old crow
while a buzzard licked its beak atop the head of tricky dick nixon
while gluttonous daly ate hundreds of pigs that were his ego
while daddy-o played bop on the box
came to the bituminous breath of chicago
howlin three-million voices of pain

& this was the music:
the kids of chicago have eyes that are older
                          than the deepest pain in the world
& they run with bare feet over south side streets
shimmering with shivers of glass
razors that never seem to cut their feet:
they dance in & out of traffic
between carhorns
the friday night smells of fish
barbecue & hog maws, the scoobedoo
blues sounds of bo diddley

2.

these streets belong to the dues payers
to the blues players drinkin rot gut whiskey on satdaynight
muddy waters & the wolfman howlin smokestack lightnin
how many more years down in the bottom
no place to go moanin for my baby
a spoonful of evil
back door man
all night long how many more years
down in the bottom built for comfort

In Texas Grass

all along the railroad
tracks of texas
old train cars lay
rusted & overturned
like new african governments
long forgotten by the people
who built & rode them
till they couldn't run no more
& they remind me of old race horses
who've been put out to pasture
amongst the weeds
rain, sleet & snow
till they die & rot away
like photos fading
in grandma's picture book
of old black men & women, in mississippi
texas, who sit on dilapidated porches
that fall away
like dead man's skin
like white people's eyes
& inside the peeling photos
old men sit, sad eyed
& waiting, waiting for worm dust
thinking of the master & his long forgotten
promise of forty acres & a mule
& even now, if you pass across
this bleeding flesh
ever changing landscape
you will see the fruited
countryside, stretching, stretching
& old black men & young black
men, sitting on porches, waiting
waiting for rusted trains
silent in texas grass

In The Manner of Rabearivello
For Jean-Joseph Rabearivello, 1901—1937

on a sea without motion, a marooned
man holding a thousand skies
over his black head, that is absent of color
a sad man staked inside the blue flame
contemplates suicide
finger dips & glides, turns
yearns always to be simply more
than a chained poet with anchored thighs

night comes down with its white leopardhide
like counterpoint, wraps its pointilistic spirit around
today's wingless promise, lying
shipwrecked at the bottom of scooped out oceans

& the day vomits out without music
where dead blood drips up from the sky, eye
the earth disappears beyond it's edges

& at the bottom of liquid ice, volcanos, 1000 sharks
flashing umpteen points of a zillion dagger teeth
struggle to swim free of the mad-dog grip
of thousands of boneless skeletons
while at high noon
amongst invisible trees of his poems
in splendiferous madagascar
rabearivello hovers, like a lugubrious bird
& sings his mournful dirges of mystery

while wide-eyed children crawl beaches
of their terrifying imaginations, without legs, crawl toward
a silent sea, whose horse mane waves are absent now of motion
where the day is washed red with nuclear bleeding
washed crimson by the ink of the sky in the sea
where the poet's eye is always capsizing

In Seventy-Seven Syllables

we are here in this cold space
as life locked loose to air

seeds of our singing, welded
as black days wed steep nights

moons play circular rituals
where mole clouds devour sad stars

black minotaurs bleed new blues
eat eggs, white with eclipse

where music rags the canvas
pure rhythms paint the day

in seventy-seven syllables

in a hurricane of dust morning
this man jumped sideways out of a dream
dressed in black
jumped right out of his own bleeding thumb
& standing wide-legged, in the middle
of the bone road
in the middle of a corpse, crowded road
drew a gun that shot out fast
from a a fast drooping, barrel of flesh
that reminded me of an old military man's penis
after his daily hecatombs
& after everytime he thinks about sex
shot out from the black
eye of that drooping, black barrel
sleeping gristle
where the moon crawls into hide
everytime the sun bursts, spitting down
its lasored sword-shafts of death
at high noon, on the deserts, in the fire-time
shot out into a cloud of bleached bone
fanged-night
slashing rain/time
a song decree, slithering
from a fast-drooping black barrel

transformed into a hurricane
of dust morning
like a wild-eyed cobra trying to escape
from a red-eyed, purple mongoose
who leaped out from a yellow cough
of limping smoke
weeping from the eye

of that invisible, cold barrel
leaped out into the rain/time
dressed in black
serious as a final heart-attack
serious, deadly serious, as cancer

Dream/Dance

seven wingless syllables, dance
peal across blues of chanting rivers
swim within cathedrals grown from bones
huckabuck across electric, circus tables
synchronized to unchanging faces of stone
fourteen perfect anachronisms
creep within the bleeding, dome of the soul
plunge towards the black, dead face of the sun
eclipsed by a solo of a yardbird
eleven soundless syllables, wrapped in stone
& dead from overliving, chant of living silence
weeping red tears, within the tempeate zone
between silence & obvious death
thirteen perfect deaths, cylindrically symmetrical
hang from fifty-one bleeding money trees
in washington, & thirteen perfect deaths, dance
in stone, unknown, thirteen soundless syllables
wrapped in stone   dream/dance

Birds Fly Without Motion To The Summit

when black air freezes into red heat
birds fly, without motion, to the summit

when the flag of despair is planted
deep in the heart, death rushes headlong
into the blood, & time rolls, like a tide
backwards, the hours run
slipping on banana peals

& skeletons rattle night-seeking flesh
where the dead masquerade as the living

the eyes seek heights of the sightless

where birds fly without motion to the summit
the air dressed like a clown freezes into night

Beneath The Bluest Sea

birds flap crumbling wings
beneath tailfire of metal hawks

distance deepens there
as the last deep breath blooms
from the fish-man swimming within the falling
dark void
slips away, as weary

flesh falls away
from bone, as time drops blood
into inkwells
life fills up with piranhas & sharks

& all around
the earth grows cities & commerce
poisonous upon mountainous sinking brows of edges

here
people sink into themselves
within hours, steps
flesh hangs loose fom bones

Snake-Back Solos (1979)

Out Here, Where

out here, where
the sky grows wings
the land is broad
beneath it
& everywhere eye go
deep space holds
me, within

Ghanaian Image — Song

after rain
dark trees
& ghost shadows
sit upon soft
shoulders
of cotton mist

Memory

a lone candle burns
penetrating the dark
deepening memory
& pain only
a finger thought flame
away, only to reach
out & touch it
touch it

touch it

Up Sun, South of Alaska:
A short African-American history song
For my son, Quincy Brandon Troupe

1.

slit balls hung in southern-american winds, then
when drumheads were slit, made mum by rum
& greed & songs dropped way down
around our ankles, bleeding up sun, south of alaska
swinging silhouettes, picked clean to bone by scavenger
black crows, hovering
caw-caws, razor scars, black winged crows, ripping
flesh under sun hot flights of slashing razors
crows & crows
& blues caw-caws & moans
& cold blues caw-caws & moans

then sunsets dangled voices
crowing blues caw-caws & black crowing razors, streaked
spreading silhouettes across a frying skillet
sky, like ink, when broken necks & sun-bloated bodies, blistered
deep in eclipse, as hang-nail ropes burned
crosses into soft mojo lives

rip of pendulum razors
lays open the quaking earth of flesh, moans
from blue-black blues women, dropping embryos
into the sucking mouth of quicksand—
to save them from a more terrible death
a more terrible death—
& african secret songs strapped across blood-stained shaving
blades, of glittering american razors, grinning like tongs
secret songs of sun/down flesh, karintha dusk flesh

drugged through spit, ripped
bleeding up sun, south of alaska
bleeding up sun, south of alaska

2.

glad crows & razors & ropes & bullets
crows & razors & ropes & bullets
the sad, cold legacy
& crazed, pale men, lassoing the sun out of the sky, for gold
coins & trinkets, then darkness bleeding up sun
south of alaska, crow wings covering the sky & black eyes
& their eyes, too, eclipsing the face of the sun
running, now, an invisible clock
with lasor-beamed hands
that are branding irons, burning our flesh
& flesh reduced over time, zones, to bone
dust, kissing stone & the nature of
stone is not moved by tongues
of heat entering, alone, sweet
lives in mouths, passionate meaning
sweet passionate touch of meaning

& still, we move through space towards grace
carrying a sphinx in one eye
a guitar in the other, knowing that time is always
locked in the possession of the keeper

3.

so now, son, black
roll the pages of your american eyes, son, back

black son back, roll them back black, son
back, american son black, roll them
son, way way back, son
black, back before the run ripped your flesh, here
way way back, sun
son, for the pages of your eyes carry the memory, son
when you hear them, son, they are oral hieroglyhics
blue-black pages in song fingers strum from
african griot songs, secret songs
run from strong black
fingers, strumming, american
blue black lives, as humming caw-caws

& black crows, here, transformed into eagles

no matter the blistering sun, son
no matter slit drums, tongues
we are here, alive, son
are wind-sun-music-spirit, son
are caw-caw blues razors, son

are keepers of secret guitars

These Crossings, These Words
For Pablo Neruda

where will they take us to
these crossings
over rivers of blood-stained words
syllables, haphazardly thrown together
as marriages that fall
apart, after one day

we have come this far through birdlime
space, to know nothing of time
too know nothing of the imprisoning distance
travelled, the scab-flesh hobos passed
we have most times given nothing

too the mirrors of our own, shattered reflections
stacked before us, like garbage, yeasting smells
molding, like corpses in smoldering streets

in our eyes, the guillotine
smile of the hangman
a time-bomb ticking for our hearts
our brains sad items bought, like so much gooey candy
our laugh wicked razor flashes, grinning
the party-time juba of my lai's sickening ritual
south africa's death squads of hyenas

american as germany roasting jews in ovens

& the blood-scarred wind
whipped rag, blue tag squared off with stars
that are silver bullets
& pin-striped with bones of mythologized peppermint

will not hide the corpse-lynched history, hanging there
twisting slowly, as a black man's body
silently screaming through soft
magnolia air, over
a tear-stained bride's — widow's —veil
breeze blown & fluttering
like a flopping fish when beached
in a gesture of complete surrender

we have come all this distance in darkness
bomb-flashes lighting our way
speaking of love, of passions instantly eclipsed
to come to find the corpse of freedom hung & machine-gunned
down, for the blood of a name beneath someone's flesh
(& what do we know of truth, when we have never been there
of the roots of this pain, raging like flaming klu klux klan crosses
because of flesh wrapped around names, blood connecting
rivers of john coltrane solos)

& there are times when we see
celluloid phantoms as our only possible lovers
mediarized commercials laying waste to our store bought brains
cracking up skeletons, crawling from bazooka cameras
jumping into movie & t.v. screens

times, still, when we stand here, anchored
nailed in our tracks, by silence
by the terror of our own voice & face
revealed in the unclean mirror, by the shattering
countless, murders, of our own, sad-faced, children
dragging anchors of this gluttonous debauchery
& of this madness that continues to last

From Richmond College,
Postmarked — Manhattan

from this plate-glass window
high above staten island
night closes in on the jugular vein of day
as black paint spreads down over space
of white canvas
artificial lights shimmer-dance
bogangle out of focus
tap-dance across the sound stuffed with slow moving ships
as the verranzano bridge strings out its chainlink
of stars, glittering necklace of pearls
pulsating strobes of flashing
carlights, rippling motion

& from this window, eye see across the sound's
waters, the shore of brooklyn comes alive with yellow
lights that probe deep
like glowing eyes of panthers

headlights shutter, blink, as if blinded
down freeways, carved out of blood & stolen gold
the american flag shivers, whips back, like a rope
popping its throat
hung up there atop staten island's city hall tower,
alone in the face of stone, cold winds
black hands on the white face
of the luminous tower clock
move quickly around
tracking time's destination

while under the verranzano bridge
the strung-out motion, red lights pulsate

like heartbeats of a rebreathing bag, dreams
rise & fall against the velvet darkness
blood colors, swirling images
tapestry the darkness
down at the rush-hour ferry landing
cars move like monstous bugs down long curving
rampways, headlights tongue their twin eyes
forward, probe, open up the darkness
with their bone bright, keys of light
crawl up snaking pavement
where people move in slow-fast
shuffling movement, as in an old silent movie
in black & white, dragging their day behind them
anchored to sad sack, drooping shoulders

now clean across the sound
in the other direction, towards manhattan
the eye locates the oxidized, green french woman
holding her light carved from stone, standing
in the polluted harbor
where democracy looms up in manhattan
behind her, like a gigantic circus
of sizzling lights
as night closes in its walls, like dracula
enfolding himself up in his black, sweeping cape
while all around, staten island supper smells
tantalize flaring nostrils

now, as eye am leaving
the wind dies
down, up on the flagpole, the flag hangs
limply, as black hands on the white face of the broken clock

run around the hours, fast as jessie owens
winning olympic dashes back
in hitler's germany, 1936

now panther against the dark
eye enter the ferry
slip down through the womb of its doors
like a letter being slid into an envelope

postmarked: manhattan

New York City Beggar

his body held the continence
of a protruding tongue
of a hanged man twisting & turning
in sweltering, needle-sharp heat
held the continence
of a jet plane's, high propulsion, saliva
his body swollen tight as a toilet stool
packed full of two-day-old shit
warts crawling, like frenzied roaches
over his skin of yellow fever
the texture of quivering pus

& he looked at me
with the look of a wrung-neck chicken
with that of a somnambulist
blasted by poison of thunderbird wine
his eyes, red storms, dead as lead
crow-wings raking their corners
like claws of a rooster

& his fingernails, the color of tadpoles
sought the origin of a 400 year old itch
which held the history
& secret of crushed indian bones
& of clamoring, moaning voices
of unborn black children
who were the screaming semen of castrated nigga dicks
& his look held the origin of ashes
the blood-stained legacy of sawdust on the floor
of a butcher
                    & his rasping, sawblading voice, cutting
held the unmistakeable calligraphy of lepers

who with elephantiasis feet, drag themselves across
sword blades of mad, pentagon juntas

(which is the history of reared-back cobra snakes
which is the truth of the cold game we're in)

& when he spoke to me in slow, blood time
his maggot-swarming words reeking of outhouses:
"brother, can you spare a dime?"
his spirit low as coal dust
his lifeforce drained as transparent shells of sunstricken roaches
his breath smelling of rotten fish market halitosis
his teeth looking like chipped tombstones
nicked away in a hurricane of razors

eye heard a fork-tongued capitalist
on wall street, fart & croak
(which is the history of reared-back king cobra snakes
which is the truth of the deadly game we're in)

& when eye walked away with my dime
chattering, still, in my pocket
he put a halloween leer on me & said: "thank you boss"
gave the V for victory/peace sign, cursed under his breath
& left, like an apparition
flapping his raggedy black coat
like giant crow wings in the wind

After Hearing a Radio Announcement
A Comment on Some Conditions: 1978

yesterday, in new york city
the gravediggers went on strike
& today, the undertakers went on strike
because, they said, of the overwhelming
number of corpses
stretched out on tables
in their overworked, embalming rooms
(unnecessarily, they said, because of wars
& plenty stupid killings in the streets
& etcetera & etcetera & etcetera)

sweating up the world, corpses
propped up straight in living room chairs
ensconsed at dinner tables, jamming up cars
on freeways, clogging up rivers, stopping up elevators
grinning toothless in stairwells
taking up kids space in front of t.v sets,
standing in line for bank tellers
stinking up bedrooms
in the gutters, dead as rudders
corpses, everywhere you turn

& the undertakers said they were being overworked
with all this goddamned killing going on
said they couldn't even enjoy all the money they was making
like bandits, said that this shit has got to stop

& today eye just heard, on the radio, that
the coffinmakers are waiting, in the wings, for their chance
to do the very same thing, & tomorrow & if things keep going
this way, eye expect to hear of the corpses

themselves, boycotting death
until things get better
or at least, getting themselves
together, in some sort of union
espousing self-determination, for better
funeral & burial conditions, or something
extraordinarily heavy & serious, like that

Steel Poles Give Back No Sweat
After Waring Cuney

in new york city people
cop their own posts
underground waiting on subway platforms
lean up against them
claim them as their own
ground & space

while up over ground
winds scrape the back of skies piercing
poles of concrete laced with laughing quicksilver
mirrors square phallic symbols
in their glint
of limp-dick capitalism
stone repositories for fallen
pigeon shit

below them stoned bums
scrape their lives into asphalt sleep
on sidewalks slow shuffle scabby bruised feet towards terrors
only they know
leaning underground
against graffitied steel subway poles
alone carrying their own feverish frenzy
that needed bathing long ago

& so each day here where we pass
each other waiting for love to speak
to us through everyone so slow in coming here
to cleanse our needs of these terrible wounds
scraped raw by these clawing days
leaning forward into one another

our lives touching here
these underground steel poles
propping up our bodies
flawed by breath
& annointed with scents
from wherever it is we are coming from

& can feel our flesh rubbing steel
& think the steel flesh
& tell ourselves we are not lonely here
couldn't be lonely
here in this gargantuan city
where steel poles
give back no love or sweat

Snow & Ice

ice sheets sweep this slick mirrored dark place
space as keys that turn in tight, trigger
pain of situations
where we move ever so slowly
       so gently into time-traced agony
the bright turning of imagination
so slowly
grooved through revolving doors, opening up to enter
mountains where spirits walk voices, ever so slowly
swept by cold, breathing fire
         as these elliptical moments of illusion
link fragile loves sunk deep in snows as footprints
the voice prints cold black gesticulations
bone bare voices
      chewed skeletal choices
in fangs of piranha gales
spewing out slivers of raucous laughter
glinting bright as hard polished silver nails

A Surrealistic Poem To Everyone
& No One in Particular

high above the ceiling of imagination
crescendo thunderclaps of silence
before lightning, a jagged tongue of pearls slashing
the tapestry of God's eye
totemic gongringer of cocaine spells
consummate tapdancer on the holy rings
around saturn
                    hydraulic wingbeatings
of a dehydrated eagle
laid back soothsayer
who sees the world as one grain of sand
cosmic mindsmoker of the seven skies of doowops & dewdrops
                    righteous deep sea diver

of the hot, sucking womb

this tomb-headed chronicler of the dark
secrets of the vatican
        omnipotent court jester
                of the kingdom of novacaine
stomp down choreographer of the nod & stumble
junkie ballets
scientific finder of collapsed river veins
molecular rhesus monkey of the ultimate trip of battery acid
peyote sky tripper, eater of jagged tin cans
fire swallowing termite of esoteric books
gri-gri stone eater of broken lightbulbs
bubonic triggerman of no hesitation

out here, your test-tube children, wearing
uniforms full of worthless medals, wearing tight

fitting suits with buttons popping, O club-footed dancers
of wet dream midnights

totemic gongringer of cocaine spells

all these desert-fried faces of sandstorms
chopped iguanas, rattlesnaking eyeballs swarming
with flies
                    sweating speech of buzzsaws & termites
cutting through majesty of redwood trees
halitosis night-trippers of onion & garlic breath
of toe-tappers of naked nose rubbing eskimos
bellringer of the turtle-snapping, sandpaper hole
sardine flesh rappers of cat-shit breath

whose eyes gleam sharp as piranha teeth
whose skunk smelling words reek of broken treaties
of no consequence & frivolous, blubberous intentions
you jellyfishes of short legs & knobby knees
& long, flat-footed premonitions

no doubt about it, O great gongringer
your childrens children continue to fuck up
& the brain of humankind seems most times a piss
of swiss cheese on the plate of a begger

It Is Not

it is not who or what
you see
but how you see
it. the night.
the light. woman. rhythm
of night lights going on.
off. in her face.
the smile of neon.
jewels on fingers.

the sound of ash
colliding with cotton.
the sound tears make falling
through blues. through guitar
strings. voices strummed
by silence. sweet echoes.
echoes. the gold-capped
dues of a mississippi black
man's grin. is. not who or what.
is. you see. but how
you see it. here. thin.
or otherwise. deep.

this life is.
what you make it. not
what you hope it to be.
but what it is. right
or wrong. what
it is is what
you make it to be.
it is. right. or wrong.
thin. or otherwise. deep.

a blues. or its absence.
it is. a lyrical deep singing.
a movement of rhythm
it is. a blueness
painting the night.
dissonant. the sound
of ashes. colliding
with cotton. is.
how you hear it
& feel it. is. not what.
or who. you either hear
it. or. you do not hear.
it. but it's how
you hear. is the question.
here. this poem.

that gold-capped blues
of that. that black man's grin.
mississippi. is.
what it is. the sound tears make
falling. through guitar strings.
colliding with cotton. blues.

voices echoing bones.
choices lay screaming under
water. under earth. hear. here.
the beauty is the feeling you hear.
here. chains. is not what you see.
but how you see them.
here. death. this life
is how you make it.

see it. feeling. see it. hearing.
hear this wife wedded to death.
hear her. see it. this life.
wedded to death.
see it. feeling. see it.
feeling in hearing.

this life wedded to death.
see it. feeling.
hear. it. singing.

this life wedded. to death.
this life. wedded. to death.
this neon. singing. hope.

this life. wedded to death.

The Old People Speak of Death
For my Grandmother, Leona Smith

the old people speak of death
frequently, now
my grandmother speaks of those now
gone to spirit, now
less than bone

they speak of shadows that graced
their days, made lovelier by their wings of light
speak of years & of the corpses of years, of darkness
& of relationships buried
deeper even than residue of bone
gone now, beyond hardness
gone now, beyond form

they smile now, from ingrown roots
of beginnings, those who have left us
& climbed back through holes the old folks left
inside their turnstile eyes
for them to pass through

eye walk back now, with this poem
through turnstile-holes the old folks left in their eyes
for me to pass through, walk back to where eye see
them there
the ones who have gone beyond hardness
the ones who have gone beyond form
see them there
darker than where roots began
& lighter than where they go
carrying their spirits
heavier than stone, their memories

sometimes brighter than the flash
of sudden lightning

& green branches & flowers will grow
from these roots, darker than time
& blacker than even the ashes of nations
sweet music will sprout
& wave its love-stroked language, like flowers
in sun-tongued mornings, shadow the light
spirit in all our eyes

they have gone now, back to shadow
as eye climb back out the holes of these old folks
eyes, those spirits who sing through this poem
gone now back with their spirits
to fuse with greenness
enter stones & glue their invisible traces
as faces, upon the transmigration of earth
become nailing winds singing guitar
blues voices through ribcages
of these days
gone now, to where
years run, darker than where
roots begin, greener
than what they bring

the old people speak of death
frequently, now
my grandmother speaks of those now
gone to spirit, now
less than bone

Collage

wings of snow sweep
disintegrate, slow fall
of chimney ashes
belch, through grey night
silently screaming

voices thick as molasses

blanket fluttering pavements
slide into one another
below moments
faces

ringing, like bells

Transformation

catch the blues song
of wind in your bleeding
human hands, (w)rap it around
your strong, bony fingers
then turn it into a soft-nosed pen
& sit down & (w)rite the love
poem of your life

Fourteen Lines For "Warm"

eye am combing back through my memories
with a fine, tooth comb, as if they were
so many, strands of hair

like pages, years flicking swiftly, as frames of a film

& now now eye see you & am next to you, there
little girl blue, where the blood is screaming
schizophrenia beneath my window

in the street, there in the bed, now
where your face is all wrapped tight in seduction

shadows growing wings of pain in your eyes
while eye am coming someone else is leaving
as the doors of your eyes slam shut

as this day's flames drop dead as sunsets
deep magic screws stars into our night

Three Poems to the Fine Lady in the Park

1. Magical Encounter

in central park, you move towards me
the summer day. (w)rapping balm
breezes come softly
tonguing. your loose, cotton dress, swinging cooly
caresses
                    your lyrical, seductive, body

& you are lathering my body
down. inside your glowing, magical eyes
you move through, & into, the sweet light
of my dumbstruck perception, falling
blind through trees
                         & then you are gone

like a sunset gone into sea

but eye am struck alive by the whispering, cooing
sweetness of your now invisible presence
am struck dumb
by your sundown flesh
gone now where choirs of the park whisper
& linger, like your perfumed breath
tantalizing here. kissing
my nose & my eyes,sad
so sad at your leaving

2. (Your Essence Stays. After Leaving)

your presence lingers there

where light trails off, at the edge
                              of shadows

& in a miracle
of rainbows & dazzling feathers suddenly
your absence rings in

it's sweet, chiming, of bell-tones

a pandemonium of rapture
where your beauty was

flowers, now, all over the sky

3. The Other Night

the other brandysweetened
night, eye dreamed we
was kissing so hard & good, you
sucked my tongue right on out
my trembling mouth
& eye had to sew it back in
in order to tell you about it

Flying Kites
For Nathan Dixon

1.

we used to fly rainbow kites
across skull-caps of hours
holes on blue wings
of the canvas of sinking suns
running winged eyes locked to wind
we'd unwind the kite string up & away
then run them down blue tapestry
up the sky again, then down
until a sinking sun rolled
down into a swallowing sky

2.

today, we fly words as kites
across pages of winds, through skies
as poems we shape from holy, bloody
adjectives & nouns
we loop into sound circles, ringing
like eclipse, the sun's tongue

Fireflies

fireflies on night canvas
pulsating like glowing cat eyes
climbing now from hidden places
making their way to secret spaces
they swim though the darkness
speaking a silent language
of their mute lives, torn from roots
in flux, & of their blinking lights
forming the core of their movement
transparent, they are blown around
every notion of wind shift
flickering through ethereal dark-
ness, where silence can be light:
wisdom searching for open doors

The Day Duke Raised: May 24th, 1974

For Duke Ellington

1.

that day began with a shower
of darkness, calling lightning rains
home to stone language
of thunderclaps, shattering, the high
blue, elegance, of space & time
where a broken-down, riderless, horse
with frayed wings
rode a sheer bone, sunbeam
road, down into the clouds

2.

spoke wheels of lightning jagged
spun around the hours, & high up
above those clouds, duke wheeled
his chariot of piano keys
his spirit, now, levitated from flesh
& hovering over the music of most high
spoke to the silence
of a griot-shaman-man
who knew the wisdom of God

3.

at high noon, the sun cracked
through the darkness, like a rifle shot
grew a beard of clouds on it's livid, bald
face, hung down, noon, sky high
pivotal time of the flood-deep hours

as duke was pivotal, being a five in the nine
numbers of numerology
as his music was one of the crossroads
a cosmic mirror of rhythmic gri-gri

4.

so get on up & fly away duke, bebop
slant & fade on in, strut, dance, swing, riff
& float & stroke those tickling, gri-gri keys
those satin ladies taking the A train up
to harlem, those gri-gri keys
of birmingham, breakdown
sophisticated ladies, mood indigo
get on up & strut across, gri-gri
raise on up, your band's waiting

5.

thunderclapping music, somersaulting
clouds, racing across the deep, blue wisdom
of God, listen, it is time for your intro, duke
into that other place, where the all-time great
band is waiting for your intro, duke
it is time for the Sacred Concert, duke
it is time to make the music of God, duke
we are listening for your intro, duke
so let the sacred music, begin

Four, And More
For Miles Davis

1.

a carrier of incandescent dreams, this
blade-thin, shadowman, jagged by lightning
crystal silhouette
prowling over blues-stained pavements
his life, lean, he drapes himself, his music, across edges
his blood held tight, within
he takes risks in staccato flights

& clean as darkness & bright as lightning
he reverses moments, where the sound becomes two cat eyes
penetrating the midnight hours, of moon pearl faces
lacing broken, mirrored waters
mississippi mean, as this sun-drenched trumpet-man
is mean, holding dreams high on any wind, light

his voice walking on eggshells

2.

& time comes as the wrinkles
of your mother's skin shrinks inward
the spirit flying towards that compelling
voice, light, calling
since time began, on the flip-side of spirit, you
miles, shedding placentas at each stage of your music
then go down river to explore
a new blues

the drum skin of young years wearing
long, the enigmatic search
of your music
changing. with every turning of the clock's hands
spinning your sound towards the diamond-point
in the river, lyrical, beyond edges
where light comes & goes

3.

O Silent Keeper of shadows
of these gutted, bloody roads filled with the gloomy
ticking of time-clocks, time running down these roads
around hairpin turns, turning in on itself
during luminous moments
when love is found when love was sought
O Irridescent Keeper, of rainbowing laughter, arching
music from a gold-capped grin

Of a bluesman, holding, the sun between his teeth

is where, you, miles, come from, playing roadhouse funk
funky soothsayer, of chewed-up moments played
clean, shekereman, at the crossroads of cardinal points
dropping dewdrop solos, of strut & slide
mean off into glide & stroll
talisman, hoodooing from bebop

trumpet voice walking on eggshells
mississippi river pouring from roots of your eyes

Poem For Skunder Boghassian, Painter

music drumming skies
of your paintings of poetry
miles cooking there
with long gone trane leaping
canopies of distance

& space can be canvas
bark negotiated by brushstrokes
                    of silence

ghosts evoking myth in illusions
wind-voice gongs shaping
shadows climbing from mist

signatures that echo

Ash Doors & Juju Guitars

we have come through doors, flaming
ashes, the sad witten legacy
smoldering bones, heaped in pyres, behind us

& yet, around campfires, blues people, singing
softly still, under blue-black moonlight

ash doors & juju guitars, conjuring, ancestral flights

sweet memories of shaman jujumen
cotton-eyed bands, crooning
softly, the guitar-woman stroked, enjoins

blues chanting mantras across the throbbing land

at the flight of sunlight
at the flight of sunlight

Skulls Along the River (1984)

Skulls Along the River
For my mother, Dorothy Smith Marshall ▬▬▬▬▬▬▬▬▬▬▬▬▬▬▬▬▬▬▬▬▬▬▬▬▬▬▬▬

1.

up from new orleans, on riverboats
from the gulf of mexico, memory carries
sweet legacy of niggerland speech, brown tongue, bluesing
muddy water
underbottomed spirits, crawling, nightmares
of shipwrecked bones
                          bones gone home to stone, to stone
bones gone home to stone
                                        to stone
riverbottomed, underbellied spirits

bones gone home to stone, eye say
bones gone home to stone, eye say

skulls, along the river

2.

& the faces of these faceless bones, unknown
screaming arpeggios of stitched memory, in cold light
cadences of blues
shrinking sun sprays, shrieking, with every turning
of black-boned-arms-of clocks

& it is the collected face of memory that wears
the metaphor of collected dust
the collective mathematics, of lamenting calibrations
hieroglyphics, cracking & peeling & curling in stones, dust

storms swirling around edges
bones, white as chiclet teeth in memory
cloning, the images come locked
in whatever time gives them
death there forever, forever locked in time
death there forever & forever locked
in time & inside of time

we suffer because we must
there is no other way to find beauty
there is no other way to find love
we suffer because we must
there is no other way home

to find the memory

& O, the skeletons that have passed
my cracking eyeballs, seeking true cadence
within the lamenting calibrations of music
history, rattling dice bones
on their worn out knees
the already dead, scraping earth, breath
for an even deeper death

the ultimate, transmigrating, transmuting

& O, you midnight men of peppermint moons
rooster claw soliloquys, raking at vision's corner
heroes, emerging, from sandblasted, history books
grant me leather flesh, of your weather worn, wisdom
blood-drenched gravediggers
                        anthracitic soothsayers

O mellow prophets of crushed grapes & stomped berries
                              grant me holy syllables
of your blues laced tongues, perfect eardrums
grant me sacred light of your blues
doowopping mackmen
                    grant me holy flight of your eagle -
winged life, grant me the tongue of your blues
perfect eardrums, grant me holy flight
of your eagle-winged life
O grant me the tongue, living
of your blues, perfect eardrums

3,

beginning with the formless mystery of love, now
    informing it all, cadences, its ritualized celebration
of birth, as death, as drama
    its copacetic language of blues
inside the journey back, under buzzard wings of parody
    textures realized & lost & found & lost once again
the slitting, definitive answer
of a pearl handled razor, hissing through the dark's wailing wall
mystery, of flesh
    wallowing in its own
gluttony, inside the breath of death

now, hear, the hieroglyphics of space & time, forming
sculpting in winds, from great distances, voices
shapes, down way, way low
voices, taking on colors, turning around & taking on shape
voices, spinning & taping into memory, phono-discs

changing into blurring faces, swimming
trying to breach this calligraphy
of space & time & distance
voices, down way, way low, spinning themselves
into memory, phono-discs, voices, spinning
resurrecting faces down in memory, graves
calling them up through metaphors
calling them up through song

send back now the poem to memory, the voice
further back than bone, see there, now, the polished stones
                              lifted & singing

singing, become birds that are soaring, words
their wings being the holy myths that fill up our lives
with movement, movement
now, listen to the blood burning songs, breaking through
& into our river voices of veins, climbing towards
the plateau of the heart

listen to the rains
beating against the underbelly of those stones
marking worm deep, earth bottoms, where
the narcissus of flesh

rests

listen to windtongues
drums breaking now into flames & wind, trumpet songs
opening up doorways to rivers, listen now
to hearts, listen
to rhythms of stones, beating hearts

climbing through the dark, listen
to rhythms, your soon to be
calcified, worm eatened
heart, listen now
eye say

listen now, to the dark

4.

we are the dark
are dark, stitched voices, climbing
memories, from the heart, are secret
arpeggios of spirit
flying towards the light
are voices of weeping rains, teardrops
wailing & hanging from historys eyelids
are voices clamorous in that toad squatting
city by the mississippi river
it's arms, wide spread
are the texture of slippery catfish
deep inside skulls of mississippi river
nights, born of savage sights
we come from the dark, hip voices
stitched into fabric
of razor bladed nights, we
are blues kneeling down
before that packing house, city —

wide spread arms slippery as cat-
fish, spirits climbing towards

the cracks of moonbeams
slashed light,
blues kneeling down
moonbeams climbing
towards cracks, slashed light

5.

O sweet lovers of no faces

of all races with desert bone dry eyes
of no reception
                              pain knee deep in quicksand
who give sandpaper tongues of no sweetness
to mouths, kisses, cold as piranha teeth
eyes digging scaly reflections in dirty mirrors
                                        cracked & fading

become, now, a confluence of rivers, bloodsouls
a confluence of musical faces, swimming through the blood
swimming through sundown, dusk
& again blood, the sonorous magic of elliptical
calibrations
                    spinning inside
memory discs, blood, stitched into music

O sing, now, of windprints, birds
          climbing cadences, stitched into memory
sing, now, of rapture swimming through river-veins
          the spirit of bones, bright as lightning
in blood deep, mud bed, of mississippi river bottoms

where the ancestors sing now through sleep
sing now, a bone deep rhapsody
a blues steeped in a memory of skulls

sing, now, a stone-sculpted legacy
of blues, chiseled, from cotton-picking mornings
sing now, put your voice to raising ancestors
        that we might pass through them

to the other side of spirit, to the other side of the mississippi
river & find our voice in those silent, now, in long gone
africa, sing now

sing a blues

6.

but this road back long gone, again long
gone, back again, blues
long gone, eye went back again to come forward
again, to this toad squatting city —
catfish arms widespread in slippery welcome —
come back home again
                        to these dry-bone kisses
of formaldehyde memories, eyes death ridden
as forty-five bullets

come back home, again, carrying my age strapped
on my hip, like a revolver
all my young, quicksilver years, running into this river
mississippi river, snake-back carrier of dreams

& home is wherever ancestors bones are
buried, kneedeep memories, live as dreams
become ribcages of miracles
legends, built from death
like a man holding the sun between his teeth
his smile, a dazzling daybreak, a blue-black blues man, son
of a man, who was the sun of another, man caught the sun
between his gapped teeth, sprouted wings
& flew away into the music

now, his spirit holds up the sky
dancing in the river, his smile the golden eye
                torching high, blue mornings, flies

snake-back carrier of dreams, mississippi
seven throw eleven to win at the game of dice
eye carry snake-back river of dreams on my back
river mississippi, where the raised spirits climb out of now
move beneath the arch's parabolic flight — upside down
beautiful, silver, question mark? razor's sharp
edge, of a stationary pendulum? — slashing the blue
throat, of the sky, now, turning into a skillet
fried-yellow, now, burnt into our dreams

snake-back carrier of dreams, the song climbs
out of itself, now, carrying the raised voices of ancestors
shaking riverweeds from itself, now, the voice full of voices
turns into faces, familiar to memory, dreams
spinning faces, familiar as crushed, coal dust
greets me here, now, with outspread arms that filigreeing
cobwebs drape, speak of old streets, where familiar buildings
have been removed, like the abscessed teeth from the mouth

of that old fisherman, ghoul
who used to tell me all those great stories
of the heydays of st. louis, before the scars came
before the mumbles came & he lost even his peg-legged teeth
like those abscessed buildings were lost
before he fell into senility & was pulverized
by the pendulum, swinging wrecking ball of progress
that is time, which is history's consuming fire
which is life & death, at the same time

7.

but this road that has been so long gone, now
is here, again, back, again, blues
long gone eye have come back to this muddy river
again, to this toad squatting city of catfish arms
widespread in slippery welcome
have come back home, again
to all my quicksilver memories, running
into this river, mississippi river, st. louis
snake-back carrier of dreams

river mississippi

snake-back carrier of dreams
seven throw eleven eye win
the game of dice — like winning in life —
seven throw eleven eye win, whatever
the game holds for me, now
whatever this catfished armed city holds
for me, now, eye win if only eye can

come forward while going back
at the same time, throw seven throw eleven
eye win at the game of dice & the blues

snake-back carrier of dreams

seven throw eleven eye win
   the blues, eye win the blues
seven throw eleven

eye win the blues

South Central, Vandeventer Street Rundown

to leave any house
was to smell the scent
burnt flesh scent hanging
            noxious in the air
        & to leave any house
was to know the odor
    burnt flesh hanging
like death in the air
        eye say, burnt flesh
            hanging
like death, in the air

& to know the odor
was to know
        where death came from
packing house, slaughter house
burning flesh, blues
spreading the news, 'bout death
burning flesh
spreading the news, 'bout death

& can smell it in springtime
can smell it in summertime
can smell it
seven days a week, singeing air
in autumntime, in wintertime
all the time, anytime

burnt flesh, hanging
    as death, in the air
eye say, burn flesh, hanging
like death, in the air

River Town Packin House Blues
For Sterling Brown

big tom was a black nigga man
cold & black
eye say, big tom was a black nigga man
black steel flesh
standin like a gladiator
soaked in animal blood, bits of flesh
wringin wet
standin at the center of death
buzzards hoverin
swingin his hamma called death
260 workdays
swingin his hamma named death

big tom was a black packin houseman
thirty years
eye say, big tom was a black packin houseman
loved them years
& swang his hamma like ol john henry, poundin nails
swang that hamma twenty years
crushin skulls
of cows & pigs, screamin fear
the man underneath slit their throats
twenty years
the man underneath slit their throats

big tom was a 'prentice for ten long years
watchin death
eye say, big tom was 'prentice for ten long years
smellin death
was helper to a fat, white man
who got slow

eye say, was helper to a fat, white man
who swang a hamma
till he couldn't do it no mo
so he taught big tom how to kill
with a hamma
eye say, he taught big tom how to kill

& twenty years of killin is a lot
to bring home
eye say, twenty years of killin is a lot
to bring home
& drinkin to much gin & whiskey can make
a gentle/man blow
don't chu know
eye say, drinkin to much gin & whiskey
can make a good man sho nuff blow
don't chu know

big tom beat his wife, after killin all day
his six chillun, too
eye say, tom beat his wife, after killin all day
his young chillun, too
beat em so awful bad, he beat em right out they shoes
screamin blues
eye say, he beat em so awful bad
he made a redeyed, hungry alley rat
spread the news, bout dues these black-blues people was payin
couldn't even bite em, cause of the dues these
black-blues people was payin

big tom killed six men, maimed a couple a hundred
& never served a day

eye say, big tom killed six men, maimed a couple a hundred
never in jail one day
the figures coulda been higher
but the smart ones, they ran away
eye say, the number that was maimed, or dead, coulda been higher
but the smart ones, they ran away
saved from the graveyard
another day
the smart ones
they ran away

big tom workin all day, thirty years
uh huh, sweatin heavy
eye say, big tom swingin his hamma, all right
twenty summers, outta love
eye say, big tom killin for pay, uh huh
twenty autumns, outta need
eye say, big tom dealin out murders, like a houseman
in the painyards, outta false pride
eye say, big tom drinkin heavy, uh huh
laughin loose, in taverns
eye say, big tom loose, in black communities
death fights cancel light
& big tom? he just keeps on
stumblin, all right

& twenty years of killin
is to much to bring home to love
eye say, twenty years of killin
is to much to bring home to love
& drinkin heavy gin & whiskey
can make a strong man fall in mud

eye say, drinkin to much gin & whiskey
can make a good man have bad blood
don't chu know
can make a strong man
have bad blood

big black tom was a cold, nigga man
strong & black
eye say, big black tom was a cold nigga man
hard steel flesh
& he stood, like a gladiator, soaked in animal blood
bits of flesh, soakin wet
stood, at the center, in the middle of death
sweatin vultures
swingin his hamma called death
260 workdays, for twenty years
like ol john henry, eye say
swingin his hamma named death

Poem For My Brother, Timmy
For Timothy Troupe ▬▬▬▬▬▬▬▬▬▬▬▬▬▬▬▬▬▬▬▬▬▬▬▬▬▬▬▬▬▬▬▬

we use to walk streets
of river-rhythm town, counting
cars, that passed
for nothing else better to do
warm, cold days, now packed away
in straw

& when at home, on delmar
& leonard streets, living over joe's
super maket, on weekends
would repeat from our window
the same ritual
all over again

this counting of passing cars

(you took the fords
eye took the chevrolets
but always the pimps cadillacs would win)

& from our window, on saturday nights
we would watch the drunken fights
across the street
at meyer's tavern
where people died with
ridiculous ease, from street surgeons knives

summers brought picnics & barbecues
baseball games & hot, funky parties
where we styled hard, laid off
in our bad, summer rags

& on warm, idle days
on concrete, playground courts
eye would beat the hell out of you
playing basketball, until it got dark

in winter, we would bundle up tight
in fast, shrinking clothes
bought three years before
when daddy was making money, playing baseball
in batista's cuba,
or bought when mother was working downtown
as a deskclerk, at sonnenfeld's

& on frozen, winter nights
we would fight, like two vicious alley cats
over who pulled the cover off of who, afterwards
we would sleep side by side
in the dark, in our own spilt blood
& if someone was ever foolish enough
to mess with either one of us
they had to contend with the both of us
sho-nuff righteously stomping
eleven-thousand corns on their
                              sorry asses

but time has worn away those days
as water rubs smooth, in time
                    a rough & jagged, stone

you took the blues of those days
filled with sun, dues & blood & turned them
into rhythms you played superbly

on your talking drums
before you heard the calling of your Lord, sanctified

eye took that beautiful song
you gave to me & turned it into poetry
this poem eye give to you, now

with a brother's deep, love

St. Louis Neighborhood
For Lester Bowie, trumpet player
& pianist, John Hicks

1.

night swept down there sometimes with a cape of screams
& eye remember my mother's voice, insistent with instructions
above the bedlam, instructive with the memory of ironing cords
punctuating their hissing, electrical language
popping & cutting through tense space
to (w)rite signatures across my back, like razor slashes
slitting in the name of love, in the name of love

2.

slicing imagination, quicks clean back through bone
to pick up the memory, swift as solo hits of a silent, sadist, rapist
alone, inside shadowed wings of darkness, destruction loose
& remembered
sad as a rabid dog's foam, dripping poison there

drop by foaming drop, back then when echoing homeboys
replicated themselves
& who prowled through dark, dracula fantasies
werewolk delusions, frankenstein, tanna leaves
mummified traumas, blown clean through dreams, like forty-five
bullets, their brains picked clean & reamed

until it is a seam shot through with darkness

3.

but there were collard green memories of sundays back there, too
bright, warm weekdays, where we sashayed like lace through
hours, filled with hop-scotch, rituals
carrying young feelings, splashed with colors
laidback, cool beauty, where sometimes there were those of us
who came close to the meaning of yardbird parker,
miles davis & bud powell
like you, lester bowie & john hicks
moving pass quickly what was told you both must become
became cock of the walks, playing the bright stride of trumpet
genius sliding fingers over piano keys,
gliding music to wherever
fingers cascading sounds into laughter
playing rhythms profound as hardons
& mysterious with birth & great, brass breath
music breathed over black-white, ivory keys

closing up the distance, between miles & bud

Growing Up In River Rhythm Town
(St. Louis, Missouri)

river rhythm town
under sun, moon, laughter
river blues town, filled
with blues people
doin blues, dues thangs

cycles of shinin laughter

listenin to dues sounds, everyday
of chuck berry, miles davis
little richard, thelonious monk
yardbird parker, the dells
& john coltranne

walkin the hip, walk
wearin the hip, new thangs
laid off clean as a broke-dick-dog
in the cut
chasin hot black girls down
rhythm & blues
doin the belly grind in corners
of smoke filled, red lighted
funky parties

music risin hot
between cold funk
of wall to wall partyin
black shadows

weavin, spinnin, dancin

drinkin in the sensuous beauty
of black, foxy ladies
yeah!
rubbin thrills against the pain
of imprisioned skin, screaming for release
from overworn, tight-fittin fabrics

& eye remember smiles
dazzling, as daybreak
& soft as mothers
warm, embracing eyes

eye remember love in the grass
sweating rivers from our fused flesh
eye remember thrills
eye remember smiles
eye remember love in the grass

sweating rivers from our fused flesh

eye remember sadness

eye remember st.louis
river rhythm town, under
sun, moon, laughter
river blues town, filled
with blues people
doin blues, dues thangs

& eye remember death

shattering, as daybreak

The Sky Empties Down Ice

the sky empties down ice
& winter grows quickly in your face
of crowded ashtrays

you say
you have come this far
for cigarettes, fun & a warm adventure
in bed
but your razor nails
clawing my back
tell me

another story

meanwhile, the sea whispers
rapture, on the other side of time
pigeons drop slimy
shit into your vanilla

ice cream cone

but don't get angry
                just yet

just because this moment defies
gravity, takes off & lands
just there
where a fart just left

all eye know is this:

the sky is emptying down ice

& winter is growing quickly in your face
of crowded ashtrays
in your burnt, butt-end

face of crowded ashtrays

Halloween Parade In Greenwich Village, 1978

it was the night of your funeral   mama
the ritualized mourning night of your death
& at the head of the affair
a black man selling luminous green bracelets of light
then a space man   plastic arrows flashing on & off
a richard nixon lookalike stalks in clown costume
rubber face   long curled-up harlequin
shoes   juggles silver balls
as dracula bites a young girl's neck
on bleeker street   eggheads bobbing up & down
skeletons grinning gyrating bones saxophones
wailing deep in the unreal noise
conga drums underneath the muffled night
pulsating tight runs as tambourines
rattle the drunk & staggering night

now fabulous masks pop out of the crowd
like champagne powered corks   cold-cock eyeballs
of people   sequins waving cat-tails   funny witches rake
long silver fingernails   transmit light
dance up & down fire
escapes up side walls of buildings   drowning
& saturated in rainbowed flights   colors
sight octopus like twenty-foot gondolas
of silk jitterbugging the night
as a pig in a red satin dress switches
her oversized rubber-packed poontang quivers
a trembling tall wolfman on stilts   shivers
two styrofoam black gloves
hold moon faces of two uptight men-girls
framed like twin sunflowers in their plucking fingers
a flute choir floats hythms over space & sights

two screams homos swapping spit
crossing seventh avenue south   the parade
claws traffic packed ten blocks back in the night
fugitive looking cars honk insistent anger

slide now down gyrating greenwich street
hook a left on west tenth   pass patchin place
(time keeping the heart of the energy) moving
pass jefferson market library
which used to be a church & before that
on the other side of time   the old women's clocked
high tower of detention   where angela davis once looked
down & out onto cheering molasses crowds —
old time ritualized socio-political masterbations long gone —
but where now   grandmama   & on the night of your funeral
mama   beneath the cheese-faced dial of the old
tower clock   mama   where black arms still turn around
time   but where this gigantic gyrating spider is now gripping
its eight legs around the church spire   mama
appears to make love to the bricks   mama
shivers in climax   mama   & turns
calm voices into agitated flights

now the drums move away carrying the spirit
hubbbub of the thing unrecognized   that holds us here
pass peter's backyard charcoal room
in front of which   a two-headed pig holds breasts
of a possessed dracula girl — cackling like that clawing   hissing
girl thing in The Exorcist — while the two-headed pig thing
mounts, begins humping her with a four-foot rubber penis
a sing-song man with a t.v. for a head   screams:

90

give me your money
give me all your dreams & money
eye sell sleeks cars guaranteed to fall apart in three years
eye sell sewing machines   poison eye stitch into your ears
& eyes   eye sell bona-fide illusions   packaged mannerisms
just for your own use   so give me money
give me all of your dreams & money
1984 has arrived

now the drums up ahead call us to turn   grandmama
at fifth avenue   rip van winkle on roller skates
& dressed in orange   black & purple   cruises by
sashaying   the parade laid dead up now in the cut of its own
rhythm   moves pass feathers now (above which the fine lady
from mississippi lived over once   before she moved in
with yours truly & blew her final chance of staying
a swinging bachelorette)
comes to washington square park   on top of whose spotlighted
lookalike   champs-elysee gateway   perches a red-suited devil
waving blessings   like the pope
welcoming everybody to the final destination
of this american   bacchanalia

now television cameras roll their shadow-catching eyes
prop lights splash darkness to the bone with light

a beggar drags by pre-arranged rags
two more fags in rock drag fall out with one another
scream at each other over whose tongue tastes sweeter
while a latin band warms up the square with salsa
languaging the park
spirit runners slip in & out the dark

mounting rhythms   lovers themselves into their flesh
richard nixon's lookalike juggles silver balls
bad as rubber checks
the band leaps into burning salsa
sways the people   cooks & turns passion
into joy on the very edge of frenzy
rockets go off in the skies of my eyes over
margeret's eyes   whose smile is a kiss
as a ten-foot high silk dragon with people for legs
rides by stunning night air above rhythms
the crowd is now dancing   holy inside
salsa   spirits moving away   inside themselves
while outside the park   a pale man in white lace
directs traffic with jeweled conductor's baton
rollers under his hairnet yawn open
their gulping mouths looping bleached blood arrogance

now   at the end of the strange affair   mama
the black man still jaw-jacking   selling green bracelets of light
ringing corded necks   as the wierd man with the t.v. for a head
is still screaming   as we fall out of the dying confusion
into the restaurant   volare   which means in italian to fly —
which we have — eye ease on up next to margaret
climb through the love conversation she carries in her eyes
leave the strange evening behind   mama
& enter volare's soft   candlelit   rhythms   mama
simmer the magic down & think of your great spirit
mama   kissing margaret   on the night of your funeral
mama   on this halloween night   mama
the day before you were laid to rest

Eighth Avenue Poem, Uptown

on eighth avenue
uptown, in black harlem
between 116th & 121
streets, on corners
some of the old junkies
have shot so much smack
into the soles of their feet
they could step on a dime
& tell you whether
it was heads, or, tails

Poem For "Lady Day" & Dinah Washington

there is nothing but yawning space between us
now, "lady day" & dinah washington
queens of the blues, your memories breaking stillness
here, the octaves of your genius voices cold-blooded
where silence reconstructs itself into pregnant punctuation
slides between chords, a hesitation of sound, arrested, perhaps
like speech of a revolutionary nailed to a star
your memories slurred & bent around
your sicknesses, filling us with omens we know
& is nothing but indigo-blues stabbed through with light
& the silence, deepening, between us now, here, where
we listen for both of you with sorrow, to hear
your voices of broken necks, twisting notes
of black men, lynched, slurred through your muddy
syllables, flowing like the mississippi river
over bright bones black flesh use to wrap itself around
once, your dead on the money voices of highways & night
trains, blue with dead men & heroin & no money
down, never, cold men you laid your jewels down on
pimps who held the secret of your voices in gin
bottles & whatever else it took to keep you singing
filling the awesome silence of rooms with your beauty
now, the octaves of your painful voodoo scaling —
silence, again, reconstructing itself, here, between
chords — stillborn in the indigo absence of your flesh
your influence punctuating in the way phrases
slide & bend, hoarse around chords, becoming
syllables waving themselves into song
the image of your memory lingering here
full of omens, like your sorrow, like your sad
beautiful faces rooted in this american apocalypse
of blues, rooted in this american apocalypse
of stone-cold, nail-you-to-the-cross, blues

New York Bag Lady

surrealistic, harlequin lady, bagging your way
through subways & streets, shocking
your shuffling, demeanor, boisterous with calamities
packed tight in your cellophane suitcases, torn shopping
bags, what do you carry in there, in your cobwebbed
memory, mama, streaking
your eyes of peppermint lightbulbs
of raked glass swimming in livid red sockets
screwed into black ringed holes
crow wings clawing at corners, speak
of journeys broken as american dreams

when eye see you there all wrapped & decked out
in your three woollen coats, inside summer's furnace
in your hand-me-down-goodwill
scarecrow rags, leaden feathers & your three-year-old-pee smell
of no money & no hopes & no place to lay down your ravaged head
your speech ventilated, savaged by God only knows what
all this madness means
your long, witch's fingernails, digging
& raking through air, as if you were buried alive
there, in some kind of grave, snot hanging like a lynched person
from your red, bulbous nose

eye think of what lost could have lead you here

woman, mama, somebody else's woman, mama
you carry defeat around in your broken-light-bulb-eyes
locked up in your mummified brazenness of ridiculous scenarios
like a diabolical comedy
you carry around tears of drowned roaches
in spider corners of cheap port bottles

your freshly slaughtered pig's face, screaming
veining inside your cutting to the bone, carnival laughter

when eye see you here all wrapped up inside
these broken dreams of americana madness, eye know
you speak to something terrible within us all, the terror
of really living inside this dog eat dog

savage, american, world

Impression #8

american lawrence welk
saturdays
            football games
hot dogs & falstaff beer
        chased by fire of bourbon

boilermakers

mcdonalds & a&p
sears   bank of america
crackers
        in chicken noodle soup
ivory snow liquid
miss america   kentucky fried
chicken   palmolive   dove
commercials

madison avenue
cowboys
            hillbilly   black
militant japtalians
niggindians   hungericans
mestizos   mulattoes

quadroons posing as white people

here   dig slick styling hip
spirits of the greased way   highsigning
give high & low fives   of speech
step the low road
strut   bojangle
their words in motion

prancing old jive   say   "gimme
some skin & lay a fin on me"
confronting soda   crackers
in this gumbo
soup   chaos of conflicting
dreams of this   what
somebody told me

was what it was all about

this american
soup of chaos   this
conflicting gumbo of

american dreams

Impressions # 12

buck dance antlers frozen
in the still, cold air
like fingers, gripping death
by the side of the crooked road
a young deer, dropped down
in its tracks, on its knees
assumes a praying position
a bullet hole in the middle
of its shocked, forehead

Impression # 15

bright day in pennsylvania
steel blue
                    the mountains clear
from here & out hear cold
the naked sky
soft at duskglow, when the sun sinks
clear down

through winter trees bare
skin leaves shake down

                    snow mounds cover
the ground & footprints
like inked words on white pages
print themselves
into sheets of snow

stretch themselves around
& into the dark, awesome
silence, grows here
into this
terrible world

Just Cruisin & Writin

writin poems
while cruisin
at seventy miles
per hour
on the pennsylvania
turnpike
can be spiritual
fun, if you don't
run into any
one.

Graveyard Humor

eye wonder why most fans
in most black churches
always have names of funeral homes
on their cardboard backs – must be
somebody's tryin to tell
black folks something

Time Opens Up

time opens up
for us, these roads
they go, falling
like stones
over sides, edges
of mountains:

people follow

Riff

may days bring an explosion of music
bouncing off edges, walls, poly rhythms
cocaine speeding through brains, carwrecks
nodding sad junkies seducing daddy death
swinging around corners, cool breezes
floating, touching everything
& sweet love left whispering now, new shadows
crisscrossing electric connections, tucked away
in memory, winter yielding cold, & spring
resurrecting all things possible, here
& the sun laughing, always on the run

Rumors

here we go again, sorting out rumors
of who did what to who & when
like, was the blind man collecting change
for real a cia agent in disguise, was he really
bruce springteen gone broke after oil cutbacks
affected all the record companies
& did so & so go to bed with so & so's wife
& have the mad, rabid pentagon men in washington
built death rays & put them into our loved ones
orbiting moons & is ronald reagan really a mummy
looking for the fountain of youth, somewhere in el dorado
florida, perhaps, somewhere in camp david's mountain
water, so old ronny can run again, play the "gipper", again
perhaps, something is wrong here
with everything we touch, we seem to fuck up
people nailing gold coins into their eyes for wall street
analysts to see them better, recognize their conformity, perhaps
put a dead rat in their cold, empty pots, perhaps sizzle them
in pac-man computers, here we go again
inventing nothing out of nothing
celebrating clones, the illusions on television
here we go again putting out rumors as sho-nuff truth
like good old boys jesse helms & strom thurmond really love
black people & homosexuals, like they say they do
have nothing against anybody unlike them
& that martin luther king is still alive & kicking
& oswald acted alone in killing president kennedy
& freedom is alive & kicking right around the corner

Memos & Buttons

he couldn't even spell albuquerque
 had tuna fish, garlic breath
mixed in with cigarette blues & a job way beyond
his zero capacity
he was a bona-fide ten martini man over lunch
same exact thing during rush hours
walking around with a copper wire for a brain
someone was sending
morse code to

he was a modern, straight man of technology
read the wall street journal & forbes religiously
every day, commuting
on suburban trains holding spit-shine images cloning himself
locked in & gigging for xerox, texas instruments, ibm
hadn't read a deep book
in God knows when
computer printouts being his bible

found himself thinking one day
of murdering his invalid wife, widowed
mother & three, teenaged children

he was a modern, western man of technology
who carried his mind around locked up
in a leather brief case

liked to push memos & buttons

Poem Reaching For Something

we walk through a calligraphy of hats slicing off foreheads
ace-deuce cocked, they slant, razor sharp, clean through
imagination, our spirits knee-deep in what we have forgotten
entrancing our bodies now to dance, like enraptured water lillies
the rhythm in liquid strides of certain looks
eyeballs rippling through breezes
riffing choirs of trees, where a trillion slivers of sunlight prance
    across
filigreeing leaves, a zillion voices of bamboo reeds, green with
    summer
saxophone bursts, wrap themselves, like transparent prisms of
    dew drops
around images, laced with pearls & rhinestones, dreams
& perhaps it is through this decoding of syllables that we learn
    speech
that sonorous river of broken mirrors carrying our dreams
assaulted by pellets of raindrops, prisons of words entrapping us
between parentheses - two bat wings curving cynical smiles

still, there is something here, that, perhaps, needs explaining
beyond the hopelessness of miles, the light at the end of a
    midnight tunnel —
where some say a speeding train is bulleting right at us —
so where do the tumbling words spend themselves after they have
    spent
all meaning residing in the warehouse of language, after they have
    slipped
from our lips, like skiers on ice slopes, strung together words linking
themselves through smoke, where do the symbols they carry
stop everything, put down roots, cleanse themselves of everything
but clarity — though here eye might be asking a little to much of any
poet's head, full as it were with double-entendres

still, there are these hats slicing foreheads off in the middle
of crowds that need explaining, the calligraphy of this penumbra
slanting ace-deuce, cocked, carrying the perforated legacy of bebop
these bold, peccadillo, pirouetting pellagras
razor-sharp clean, they cut into our rip-tiding dreams carrying
their whirlpooling imaginations, their rivers of schemes
assaulted by pellets of raindrops
these broken mirrors catching fragments
of sonorous words, entrapping us between parentheses
two bat wings curved, imprisoning the world

Las Cruces, New Mexico
For Keith Wilson, Donna Epps Ramsey, Andrew Wall
Charles Thomas, Thomas Hocksema
& the Indian who told me much of this

the high, great mesas, flat as vegas gambling tables
rock-hard, where red dust swirls into miniature tornadoes
dancing down roads red with silence
as these faces of solitary indians here, where white men quick
tricked their way to power, with houdini bibles, hidden
agendas of bullets & schemes of false treaties
& black men alone, here, in this high, stark place of mesquite
bushes, white sand mountains, colors snapped in incredible beauty
eyes walking down vivid sunsets, livid purple scars slashing
volcanic rock, tomahawking language
scalping this ruptured space of forgotten teepees
so eye listen to a coyote wind howling & yapping across
the dry, high vistas of cactuses, kicking up skirts of red dirt
at the rear end of quiet houses, squatting like dark frogs
& crows, etched silhouettes high on live wire

popping speech, caw-cawing, in the sand-blasted wind-stroked-trees
                    caw-cawing all over the mesilla valley

& here along the rio grande river, parched, dry tongue bed, snaking
cracked mud, dammed north in the throat of albuquerque
mescalara, apache, navaho & zuni live here
scratch out their fire water breath, peyote secret eyes roaming
up & down
these gaming table mesas, their memory dragging chains through
these sun torched streets
while geronimo's raging ghost haunts
their lives with what they did not do, stretching
this death strewn history back to promises

& hope a hole in the sky, a red omen moon
where death ran through like water
whirlpooling down a sink

& this jade shaman moon blown here a target of light
at the end of a tunnel of blackness, where a train speeds through
now, towing breaknecking flights of light, where daybreak sits
wrapped, like a blanket around the quiet
ancient navaho, wrapped in cosmic, american colors
who sits, meditating, these scorched, flat, white sands

distant high mesas shaped like royal basotho hats
chili peppers, churls, pecan groves, roadrunner chaparral birds
salt cedars, sprouting parasitic, along bone white, ditches bordering
riverbeds thirsting for water
meditates these flat, wide black, lava rocks
holding strange imprints of fossilized speech that died
before they knew what hit them, as did those silent clay faced
ancestors of this solitary navaho, sitting here wrapped
in breaking colors, bursting sunlight
meditating the lay of this enchanting blues
land, changing its face every mile or so

& in their faces indians carry the sad betrayal of ancestors
who wished they had listened to those long gone
flaming words — battlecries — of geronimo, whose screaming ghost
prowls these once bloody streets, baked dry & quiet now
by the flaming eye torching the sky,
wished they had listened to instead of chaining
his message in these coyote, howling winds
kicking up skirts of dirt

whose language yaps & flaps, like toothless, old men & women
back at the rear-end of quiet houses, whose lights dance slack
at midnight, grow black & silent as death's
worn-out breath, beneath these pipe-organ mountains
like bishops peaked caps
holding incredible silence, here
in the mesilla valley

where the rio grande river runs dry
it's thirsty spirit dammed north in the throat
of albuquerque, at the crossroads of fusion & silence
in the red gush swirls — whispering litanies sawblading through
ribcages, dust memories — snaking winds all over the mesilla valley
brings long gone words of geronimo, haunting
las cruces, new mexico, long gone wind, whispering

geronimo, geronimo, geronimo

It All Boils Down

it all boils down to a question
of what anything is done for
in the first place
a reason, perhaps, for the first recognition
of clouds, cruising through seas of blue
breath, shaped like battleships

on the other hand
it could be a fascination wearing rings
on sweating, clawing fingers
something we have forgotten
perhaps, something we knew nothing about, ever
like the future of a question only time holds
answers to, such as the exact moment
death puts a lean on
flesh, perhaps
& the thin suit vanity wears
collapses it on itself
as the spirit takes leave of breath
& voices swell into a cacophonous blues

mother, somewhere in all of this
there are connections, fusing, something
perhaps, in the mellifluous nodding of crazed junkies —
that sad, leprous colony of popeye hands & feet — is a dance
a catatonic premonition, of unheeded weather reports
like the knowing somewhere deep
that eclipsed suns will perhaps experience joy
in the shaved light —

a shopping list of syllables is what poets carry
when confronting the winds of language —

like evil laughter, gleaming machetes swing under streetlamps
slicing quick words that cut a man too short to shit
sometimes, perhaps, it is this
or a concertino stream of blue ragas
when breath flies suddenly back here, mysterious
as in those moon glinting eyes, fixed in silence
the dime-polished speech of felines
in a midnight moment of celebration

a bone dry, squawking hawk talking away up there
suddenly, beyond dues, disappearing into blue quicksand
flapping wings of unanswered questions

down here, on earth, it all boils down to questions
ribcages pose & leave scattered under terrifying suns
on desert floors, the timeless, miraging sands, holding
light, the steaming, seamless language
in flight & flowing into midnight

these moons climbing between me & you

116th Street & Park Avenue
For Pedro Pietri & Victor Hernandez Cruz

116th street fish smells, pinpoint la marqueta
up under the park avenue, filigreed viaduct
elevated tracks
where graffittied trains run over language
there is a pandemonium of gumbo colors stirring up
jumbalaya rhythms
spanish harlem, erupting
street vendors on timbale sidewalks
where the truth of things is what's happening now
que pasas on the move, andale
worlds removed from downtown, park avenue gentry
    luxury coops
where latino doormen just arrived, smile their tip me good
    tip me good, tip me good, greetings
opening doors
carry their antediluvian, rice & bean villages, old world
style, dripping from zapata moustaches
shaped perfect as boleros
their memories singing images underneath shakepearean
cervantes balconies, new world don juans
smelling of cubano cigars, two broken tongues
lacing spanglish up into don q syllables, bacardi
cuba libre thick over sidewalks
voices lifted & carried up into dance
up into mambo-cha cha slick steps, these bodies
imagine themselves out on ballroom floors
rumbling car horns, machito fused, pacheco tuned
palmieri fired, barretto drums
bolero guitars wiring morse code puns
root themselves back in villages
    of don juan, omeo, zapata

marti writing poetic briefs in cuba
   under cigar trees, the lingua-franca
of guillen, morejon, cruz & pietri
laying down language of what's happening now
& weaved through this pandemonium of gumbo
colors up under
the park avenue, feligreed
viaduct, crisscrossing 116th street
smell, pinpointing la marqueta
where elevated trains track over language
run over syllables up on elevated tracks, fuse words
(w)rap lyrical que pasas on the move, andale
   spanglish harlem
nuyorican sidewalks, exploding fried bananas
   timbale shopping carts up into salsa
sweat new borinquen slick steps
buzzard winged, moustached, newyorican muchachas
in a new world black latin groove, at the crossroads
where the truth of things is what's happening now
the truth of thing's is what's happening, now

A Poem For "Magic"
For Earvin "Magic" Johnson, Donnell Reid & Richard Franklin

take it to the hoop, "magic" johnson
take the ball dazzling down the open lane
herk & jerk & raise your six feet nine inch
frame into air sweating screams of your neon name
"magic" johnson, nicknamed"windex" way back
   in high school
cause you wiped glass backboards so clean
where you first juked & shook
wiled your way to glory
a new style fusion of shake & bake energy
using everything possible, you created your own space
to fly through — any moment now, we expect your wings
to spread feathers for that spooky take off of yours —
then shake & glide, till you hammer home
a clotheslining deuce off glass
now, come back down with a reverse hoodoo gem
off the spin, & stick it in sweet, popping nets, clean
from twenty feet, right-side

put the ball on the floor, "magic"
slide the dribble behind your back, ease it deftly
between your bony, stork legs, head bobbing everwhichaway
up & down, you see everything on the court
off the high, yoyo patter, stop & go dribble, you shoot
a threading needle rope pass, sweet home to kareem
cutting through the lane, his skyhook pops cords
now lead the fastbreak, hit worthy on the fly
now, blindside a behind the back pinpointpass for two more
off the fake, looking the other way
you raise off balance into space
sweating chants of your name, turn, 180 degrees

off the move, your legs scissoring space, like a swimmer's
yoyoing motion, in deep water, stretching out now toward free
flight, you double pump through human trees, hang in place
slip the ball into your left hand
then deal it like a las vegas card dealer
off squared glass, into nets, living up to your singular nickname
so "bad", you cartwheel the crowd towards frenzy
wearing now your electric smile, neon as your name

in victory, we suddenly sense your glorious uplift
your urgent need to be champion
& so we cheer, rejoicing with you, for this quicksilver, quicksilver
                                             quicksilver
moment of fame, so put the ball on the floor again, "magic"
juke & dazzle, shake & bake down the lane
take the sucker to the hoop, "magic" johnson,
recreate reverse hoodoo gems off the spin,
deal alley-oop-dunk-a-thon-magician passes
now, double-pump, scissor, vamp through space
hang in place & put it all up in the sucker's face, "magic"
johnson, & deal the roundball, like the juju man that you am
like the sho-nuff shaman man that you am
"magic", like the sho-nuff spaceman, you am

Leon Thomas, At The Tin Palace

eye thought it was the music, when
in fact, it was a blender
grinding down ice
making stuffings for drinks, but then
you jumped right on in, on the downbeat, leon
jumped right on in, stroking rhythm, inside time
inside the bar, then

people flew deeper into themselves
became the very air sweeping language to crescendo
between feathers of touch, looping chord changes
your voice blued down, blues cries, field hollas
mississippi river, flooded guttural
stitches through your space
images of collective recall, leon

your voicestrokes scatting octaves —
the ice grinding down still inside the blender
making stuffings for pina coladas — then
you scooped up our feelings again
in the shovel of your john henry doowops, leon
jazzed through ellington, count & bird
yodeling coltrane, blues cries
the history of joe williams
sewn into the eyes of our eardrums
transmitted to the space, between the eyes
where memory lies

your scatting licks brings us back dancing
in our seats, you kick, swelling language, inside
your lungs, voice stroking colors
painting the Creator's masterplan

as pharaoh explodes inside the tone blender of his horn

the ice grinds down, the bar jumps out of itself
scooped up in the shovel of your john henry doowops
blue, as a mississippi river chord, gutteral phrasing
flooded, octaves kicking back black
scatting rhythms, loop, busting your chops

feather stroking phrasing, leon thomas
yodeling octaves, chords sewn back black

where they came from

eye fall asleep in order to dream a poem awake
it comes surreptitiously, sometimes it balks
holds back its mystery
so much so, sometimes, it reminds me of pulling teeth
or a roundabout, sly, back-door man
who is afraid of sunlight

sometimes poems come, like easy women
a fine-to-the-bone, supple, long-legged flash through
slit silk the wind licks open, to tease-tongue
a marvel of flesh
words, sometimes, come like that
sometimes flying around the sun, in blurred lines
like moths, frenzying around lightbulbs
words gather themselves into tribes
stanzas, held together by ritualized process
they stitch together threads of syllables
into rhythmic, associated sounds

sewn deep connections, like veining family
blood, these poems eye dream awake
the images — shaped by these word-takes
when stitched together by rhythm, silence & space —
the sun shining through them
the threat of fired bullets, love, the moonface
grace of another place

Birds Ski Down

birds ski down the day's inscrutable smile
wheeling, they bank their diaphanous
voices sawblading, their sword-like, sleek feathers
cutting through the day's upper reaches of silence
their convoluted lanuage, cacophonous
& raucous as a lynch mob
in old georgia, the rope-rasping cutting of their burning
syllables, hanging there, twisting their meanings around
us & these blooming, dark hours of spring
stormy with the chaos april brings
suddenly upon us —
like a black panther, clawing away
our breath — this changing day suddenly filled
with so rare & mysterious a beauty —
like these wheeling birds thrill us —
it thrills us to death

Male Springtime Ritual
For Hugh Masekela

it's hard on male eyeballs, walking new york streets
in springtime, all the fine, flamingo ladies
peeling off everything the hard winter forced them to put on
now, breasts shook loose from strait-jacketed, layered clothes
tease invitations of nipples
peek-a-boo through see through, clinging blouses
reveal sweet things our imaginations need to know to fire mystery
they jelly-roll, seduce through silk, short-circuit connections
of dirty old men, mind in their you-know-what young men, too
they fog up eye glasses, contact lens, shades —
& most of these sho-nuff hope to die lovers
always get caught without
their portable, windex, shade-cleaner bottles
& so have to go blind through the rest of the day
contemplating what they thought they saw

eye mean, it can drive you crazy, walking behind one of those
memorable asses in springtime, when the wind gets cocky
& licks up one of those breeze-blown, slit, wraparounds, revealing
that grade A, sweet poontanged, rump of flesh & it is moving,
deep, like those old black african ladies taught it to do, & do
eye mean, it's maybe too much for a good old boy, staid, christian
chauvinist, with a bad heart & a pacer
eye mean, what can you expect him to do —
carrying all that kind of heavy baggage around —
but vote for bras to be worn everyday & abolish any cocky wind
whose breezy tongue gets completely out of hand
lifting up skirts of young, fine, sweet thangs
eye mean, "there ought to be a law against some things"
eye'm sure he would say, "reckless eyeballin'"

eye'm sure he would say

anyway, it's hard on menfolk streetwalkers in springtime
liable to find your eyeballs roaming around dazed
in some filthy, new york city gutter
knocked there by some dazzling, sweet beauty, who happened along
your limited, field of vision — who knows, next thing you know
they'ill be making portable pacers for eyeballs —
& who cares if you go down for the whole ten count
& never pull your act back together again

& so become a bowery street bum, a dazed babbling
idiot, going on & on about some fine, flamingo lady you thought
you saw, an invitation, perhaps
& who cares if her teasing breasts shook you
everwhichaway, but loose

it's springtime, in the old big apple
& all the fine, flamingo ladies, are peeling off
everything the hard winter forced them to put on
their breasts shake loose from overcoats
tease invitations of nipples

it's all a part of the springtime ritual

& only the strongest eyeballs, survive

A Poem For Lynne
For Lynne Edwards

eye drape my shadowing body over your body —
a black eagle's wing inking nutmeg flesh —
taste the music of your sweet tongue
a blue lyric from the sun skies down, closing gates
over your eyes, which remind me of smiles pearls bring
to crease faces of deep-sea divers, probing sand-gritty
ocean oyster shells, smiles duplicated
in warm skies of your eyes

& this moment is a spring, morning flower, opening
up, beyond the touch of wind, there are your cool, sweet
lips, which hold out the promise of succulent language
sun-stroked tongues of breezes
a lyricism, talcum soft & cushioning as your kissing mouth
eye (w)rite into this poem, mysterious as the origins of feathers
bird wings tracking lifeprints, nailing holes in the roof of skies
bright blue, high murmurings
as in the in & out breathing of your rhythm

hip deep & turning around its own energy
eye taste live-wire music of your sweet tongue, now
this moment, like a flower, opening up to spring morning,
touching
sun-stroked language of breezes
duplicated feather glide of birds, your eyes banking
coals stroked into words & sewn whispering into this sky's poem
as when sunsets linger, trembling footsteps over water
your smile breaking quick as lightning in skies
of your feather-stroked, sundown eyes

your touch, dew-drop syllables, full of sweet breezes

tonguing this moment, a spring flower opening up
beyond promise, beyond sun-stroked winds
my eagle shadow draping over your nutmeg body —
a black wing spreading flags —

over your lyrical, so luminous, body

Eye Throw My Rope Tongue Into the Sky

eye throw my rope tongue into the sky
send out words of love, lassoing to you cross
blue valleys of distance
fight off swirling tornados, desert fried
fools, who want to intercept this message for you
only for you, rain-swept, cooing lady, wooing
tongue of cool, soft rain, soothing
my voice, a wing of stroking feathers
riffing & riding the hot wires, comes tickling
your eardrums, my sweet tongue, looping lyrical
melodies of fire, wet, sound waves
my rope tongue looping, melodies cross skies
comes tickling, poetically, your eardrums
in wet sound waves, sweet sound, waves

A Thought for You, Margaret
For Margaret Porter

eye stretch my lips, 3000 miles
cross telephone wires, sucking silence of wings
beating down breath, space
      a hemorrhaging of distance

& you there singing as dusktones, in the apple
rainbow feathers, sleeping there, as loveliness, peace
& we have come to this magic apart from each other
ourselves alone with distance

serene inside this breathing music

muted trumpet voice kissing fabled dusk song
skin of scarred history, long distant embraces in dreams
memory easing out of breath
rhythms gliding in & out, over & under
like birds — banking feathered wingprints —
wheeling down sunset skies

& now your love call coming through
clear, the night wind's sucking, deep mystery
through space, black distance collapsing in
on itself, screaming, so beautiful
the grip of your sonorous name, soothing

so soothing, the tongue touch, of your sonorous name

A Poem For Ojenke & K. Curtis Lyle

if, in a comatose instant of deep listening
you should come across a syllable
wide as the sky of pure hearing & sleep
as whenever anytime your eyes carry themselves
to their limits of recognition, crystal, as on a steel blue
day of bright, clear winter
at the moment of that rare clarity
as in the listening to a black, blues band
steeped in the bone & blood utterance of gut-bucket
bucket of blood tradition, if — eye say if — in the stop action
freezing of a negative snapped image heard & fashioned
there from that sound you just perceived now in the knowing
of that terror, just now, there, gutteral, as in the whiskey
broken voice-life of ma rainey, chained
to microscopic grooving of a vinyl instance
recorded then full of all things considered meaningful
there — then, as now, it's all about choices —
what it all means when everything is left hanging out there
in the cold, like blood-splattered sheets billowing under
a lolling, blue light, an enfolding, cool blue rinsing
morning that now switches up under a chameleon sun
to heat, now, like cynical laughter
sweating down rivers of gold light beamed there
& if, in the rifle sighting focusing of that clearly cold
instant, comatosed, you should happen across a syllable
wide as the sky of new hearing & blue deep
blue deep, as where anytime your vision carries itself
to the limits of recognition, if you should hear a crystal
song ringing out there & during that moment
of rare, pure clarity, a voice, perhaps
a note, like a breeze, fluting over & informing
this moment, perhaps, like a cool, blue morning, rinsed

folding over a beginning poem, there
& in the crystal clear hearing of that moment
& in the bone & blood spirit of gut-bucket blues
tradition, & if you should hear a new crystal image
there, call me with a poem, great & good brothers
call me singing & call me, through a poem

Conjuring Against Alien Spirits
For Ishmael Reed

if there is something that takes you
to the brink of terror
turn your pockets inside out, like a lolling dog's
tongue, salivating, in heat, make a screech-
owl's death cry go away, go away
make a screech owl's death
cry go away, go away

turn shoes upside down at your own
front door, tie a knot in your apron string, mama
sister, throw fire on salt
talk to raw head & bloody bones
make a hoot owl screaming death
go home, take it away
make a hoot owl take it away, on home

turn your pillowcase inside out
see a cross-eyed, devilish fool, cross
your fingers — drop goobadust in your mind medicine
eat a root doctor's magic root — spit on them, sho-nuff
make a cross in the road
where you met yourself coming
& going, spit on it

that same spot, where you passed over
just now, in the road, spit on it, to soften up enemies
walk backwards, along any road you have passed over
before, a red moon, like a one eyed wino's stare
stuck in bone shadowed trees, there
throw dirt over your left shoulder
spit down on it, in the road

spit down on that same spot
where your terror locked into itself
locked into another enigma
where someone's footprints leave their signatures
of weight, define shapes of worn soles
speak to raw head & bloody bones
great-great-great grandmama
make a hoot owl screaming death

take his case all the way home
screaming, all the way home
make a hoot owl screaming death

take your death slip, all the way home

evenings rise here with voices of old people
whispering up sky, a cat-eyed moon riding
wings of bat syllables, rising
brushing up against mystery, eyelids of language
winking their hushing rhythms through serenading trees
xylophones, carrying cooling winds to memory
couch their soothing sounds, in magic of primeval wisdom
the orchestration of harmony, between ensembles of birds
whose voices whisper, riffings up steep skies
carrying history, a lynx-eyed moon rides up on
rising, like muted tongues of old people
ventriloquists of southern nights
whispering, there, on porches
cobwebbed shadows inside filigreed
half light, the old peoples lilting voices
yeasting with wisdom in their sundown
eyes, riding up sky, longside a lynx-
eyed moon, wings of bat syllables
soothing, a xylophone, a tune

Passing On the Legacy
For Henry Dumas & my son, Quincy Brandon Troupe

we stand here, within these bones
within our spiritual selves, breathing within
flesh of these years, melting like ice cubes
in drinks
within stone, these thoughts
these miracles of roots found inside
our folklore, these links stretching four hundred years
back to villages eaten black by halloween flames
eating up the dark, rhythms, rhythms
eating up the dark
                    rhythms, rhythms

& here, weaving shadows, dance through
leaves, stretch to hear, across atlantic, salt water
the bugaman high in trees
listens to the drummer's shaping hands

& time breaks wind & bone down to nothing
stone, also, juxtaposed next to feathers

& there aren't too many secrets
these days that are not known, we speak
through our eyes, speak
& see through our ears & tongues
& hear through our tongues

& so we stand, within tone of these bones
inside these years, ringing, like bells
a coltrane solo, solo

& now eye reach out the smile

of my tongue, blue-black with rhythms
reach out my tongue
a jazz-blues riff of dues payments
reach it out to you, a love gong
chiming from my eyes
hand over to you, my oldest son
this signature born in blood & fire
& baptized deep in river-bottoms
hand over to you
this sun toned hardness

this guitar full of lives

so, take the vision, brandon
& run up sun with it
look back into your own eyes

for you are the memory
carrying the future

New Poems (1984 - 1990)

Changing Course ▬▬▬▬▬▬▬▬▬▬▬▬▬▬▬▬▬▬▬▬▬▬▬▬▬▬▬▬

suddenly, as in the breaking up of an old love affair
eye feel this urgent need to change course
my poetry's compass point, my pointer dog
words, celebrating tombstones, like a virtuoso of graveyards
eye have always thought of blood & gore as holy food for metaphors
the black holes of dead eyes, strung out through space
a kind of holy grail, always stitching through my poems
was what my poems required, death here the glue
that held my coffin shaped stanzas, together
death, a kind of grace in the poet's eye

& eye thought this was the way to reach holy, poetic transcendence
the only sacred place to lay my free verse, blues head down in
as in a casket, billowing bright silk, pillowing & cushioning, my
   words
than quicker than quick, eye fell in love with wind music, sweet
   singing
of birds, wooing through trees in the west indies
leaves greener, more lasting than american money
fell in love with gold flecks on the blue/green sea
fell in love with beauty surrounding me

that's why eye felt the need to change poetic direction, perhaps
try & resurrect a long dead humor
maybe, write some poems about my missing front teeth
how they remind me of inverted, football goal posts, a yawning,
wide open doorway, perhaps, my gap-tooth smile, welcoming
hiphopping roaches & flies, who are as homeless as some
people might be, maybe, something like that might tickle
somebody's funny bone, like a poem about my son's pleading
socks, stiff with absolute funk & toejam, might tickle

after attacking nostrils, like screaming banshees
maybe, something like that, might take me away, perhaps
back to some healing laughter, eye want to dress up in
my poems, with sidesplitting wisecracks
perhaps an image of a one-legged, drunken midget
trying to dunk a basketball, over air jordan or larry bird
might do, who when jumping only raises a hickey
on a mosquito's kneecap, sitting on a turd

maybe, eye should try writing something about the humor of fucking
perhaps, something truly lowbrow like that will do wonders
will be just what the doctor ordered

about how the first time eye tried to do it eye was frightened
how eye thought eye would die of something sinister
believing, as eye did then, that fucking violated the athlete's pure code
that eye should refuse to enter that sweet, seductive hold of love
that it was certainly corrupting to flesh
(& if eye did it - - which eye eventually did - -
that God would surely strike me deader than a rusty nail
hammered into the cowboy humor of old chicken neck, ronald reagan
perhaps, eye could hang my words on that) & how after eye finally did do
it how eye missed that wondrous, whirlpooling grip, the first time around
& how after eye finally found it, eye found it so hypnotic
& thought eye was peeing when eye was busting my first nut
& so ran dripping & trembling into the bathroom, embarrassed
certain eye would die, shooting missiles of sperm
all over that slippery floor

maybe, something like that might get me going in the right direction

it's all so confusing, now, this sudden need to be funny
as eddie murphy, trying to make someone laugh so quakingly hard
they belch out their false, upper teeth, into their triple shot of bourbon
blowing their manicured cool all over my lines

& yet eye don't seem to know anymore who eye am
so completely confusing to me is this new, poetic direction
eye'm trying to get myself into now
eye feel like eye'm trying to fit my poems into wrong footed shoes
trying to wear brand new ones much too small & tight
their language & point of view rigid, as some corporate executives are
no jimi hendrix free rhythms pulsating here through
my new poems, soft now, as newborn, baby shit
soft now, as grunting cow moos

my new poems packed with flat-assed words of two-day-old beer

eye don't want to be confused anymore, so eye think eye'ill go back
to blood & gore, spill out my guts again in my usual graveyard,
  black humor
fill up my poems again with metaphors cold as cobra themes that bite
into pulsating, free rhythms of death & life
forget about humor, this way eye'ill be right in the flow

this way eye'ill feel absolutely comfortable

Perennial Ritual

For all the dictators of Haiti & anywhere else ▬▬▬▬▬▬▬▬▬▬▬▬▬▬▬▬

they are killing the joy of laughter once again
they're slaughtering the smiles of children
they're banning the music from language once again
they are marching in goose-steps to rhythm of bullets
they're putting cyanide in peoples drinks of hope again
they are trading back their freedom for strings of puppet money
they're digging mass graves for the innocent once more
they're cutting down trees that hold back the floods
they're macheteing roots of their bloodlines once again
they're smearing blood on their mother' faces dead as moats
they're ripping out the tongues from their history again
they're butchering all love like they would a goat

what is it they hate in themselves, in clear, new mirrors
what is the dry as bone spit of their snake-eyed fear, their terror
of bloodlines, running deep as the secrets of voodoo
what is the future they want everyone to dance through
where the poison come from flowing through their puffer-fish hearts
where their thoughts turn to after uzis shoot joy from the dark
& the eerie silent roads hold only the shadows of murderers

bufo marinus namphy, sweating beneath tunics medalled with skulls
his henchmen sitting black stone-faced with their slit cobra eyes
cool & evil prosper avril & regala, lafontant & old bossman, duvalier

what is the is the suicidal urge they pick up from other scumbags
licking out their lizard tongues cancerous with warts
their dum-dum, bazooka eyes of mamba snakes
deadly as a fart at a republican party, whose american president
     keeps them
stumbling here with his famous soft shoe, his chicken neck flapping
     clues
his glued hair plastered in place, embodying what they will sink to
what they will kill for to become

O, they're shooting out the lights of port-au-prince once again
they're turning people there into zombies with their snake-eye guns
they're trying to kill the moon in a dreamer's eyes once more
they're feeding the vacant-eyed poor with teaspoons half-filled
     with garbage
they're lining up beggars & killing their hunger again
they're goose-stepping to the rhythm of bullets

The Childen at the Throat of the Bay
For Danel George, who took me there

when we bought the roasted, haitian chicken
the children swarmed around us, like small rats
eye could imagine swarming all over the stinking
mountains of garbage
piled high, just in back of the chicken shack
gulls wheeling there, like vultures zeroing in on the dead
which most of these children already are in their heads
& spirits, their shifting eyes glinting like doberman
pinschers, smelling of rottening mud, wet with maggots
barefoot, they wear clothes black as scarecrows
& they will do anything for food, or money
in this dog eat dog, terrible, black hole
anything, their bright, sharp teeth, shining
like just polished razor blades
still, even here, some are proudly beautiful, cold
refuse to beg, plot instead of how to kill us

Boomerang: A Blatantly Political Poem

eye use to write poems about burning
down the motherfucking country for crazy
horse, geronimo & malcolm king
x, use to (w)rite about stabbing white folks
in their air-conditioned eyeballs with ice picks
cracking their sagging balls with sledgehammer blows
now, poems leap from the snake-tip of my tongue
bluesing a language twisted tighter than braided hope
hanging like a limp-noosed rope down the question mark
back of some coal miner's squaw, her razor slanted
killer shark eyes swollen shut with taboos
she thought she heard & knew
the sun in a voice looking like bessie smith's severed arm
on that mississippi back road, screaming, like a dead man's son
who had to watch his old man eat his own pleading heart
& sometimes eye wonder if it's worth the bother
of it all, these poems eye (w)rite holding
language percolating & shaped
into metaphoric rage
underneath, say
a gentle simile, like a warm
spring day, soft as balm or talcum
on the edge of a tornado that hits quicker
than the flick of a bat's wing nicking the eye

eye use to write poems about killing fools like ronald reagan
daffy duck grinning off 30 million sucked down
the whirlpooling black holes of cia space
director casey taking a lobotomy
hit, slash to protect
the gipper
dumb

motherfuckers
everywhere tying bombs
to their own tongues, lighting fuses
of staged events that lye of peace & saving
money in the s & l pirateering, like president gipper
they are metaphors for all that's wrong in america right now
all this cloning, brouhaha, paid mouthpieces on wall street
& the gipper giving frying skillet speeches, that ray gun reagan
ray gunning america, now, cannibalizing airwaves
with mouthpieces fronting slimy churches
building up humongous bank accounts
in the name of the holy bones
of jesus christ, long gone
& dead
& it is a metaphor
boomeranging jimmy
& tammy bakker, sleazy swaggert
vacuuming pocketbooks of the old & the dead
like medusa meese heads nicked off & sluicing like bad faith
they dangle heads from "freedom fighter" mouths
tell the black bird press herded up on a wire
that it's okay, it's okay,
it's okay

eye use to write poems about burning
down the motherfucking country for crazy
horse, geronino & malcolm king
x marks the spot where "coons" signed away
their lives on dotted lines, black holes
sucking away their breath
for a sack of cotton

full of woe & so
eye
sit here
now, (w)riting
poems of the soft
calm beauty welling
in my son's innocent 4 year
old eyes, thinking, perhaps of the time
when this rage will strike him, driving him towards madness
knowing all the while it will come quicker than quick
sooner than expected
& nothing
absolutely nothing
will have been undone

Les Cayes, Haiti & 3 Religions on Parade: 1984

1. Voodoo

on good friday, fronting the square
rara called the few old faithful here through
bamboo, the drum masters stroking their signatures
rooted clues deep beneath the surface, voodoo
found its medium in lulu
the lithe, loa dancer
baton twirlers, beyond the blues
that lightning spoke of in a mojo hand
a mojo hand, a sequinned loa called through
sluicing, bamboo clues, voice deep
in voodoo, a mojo hand, calling
somewhere, somehow, old
lightning hopkins knew
came close to playing
what this was all about

2. Catholicism

the catholic parade hustled many through
droves moved through the dark streets of les cayes
mixed bloods & pure bloods walking shoulder to shoulder
the crucifiction myth nailed in all their heads
nailed in their hearts,
bloods bearing up the cross through the dark
the hymns of jesus christ's blood running
through their voices up ahead, pulling
blood of three nails hammered down
through centuries of His blood

running like ribbons through these streets
reining ropes pulling His invisible image, here
through these litanies of blood
& bloody all these bodies snaking through
les cayes, full of nails driven through
open palms & feet, screaming
their bloody, burdened, invisible voices
of mythical blood flowing invisible through
these dark, narrow streets
the many faithful meet, shoulder to shoulder
mixed bloods & pure bloods, carrying
their crosses in their voices
shoulder to shoulder, snaking through les cayes
les cayes, spirit to spirit, on this good friday
evening, & all them deep in voodoo, too

3. The Protestants

the protestants were silent on this day
& perhaps their silence spoke for them, too
whatever their numbers
silence spoke this evening for them, too
who were not here

Cap Haitian
For Patrick Delatour, Monique Clesca & Bernard, our guide

tucked in the elbow crook of the bay
large ships, perched like oversized grasshoppers
rock n roll on the blue, soft waves lapping in & out
in slow motion, the old city climbs up the mountain
like an old man & woman
whose stairs are behind them
& held up on skinny bird legs, terraces poke out their lips
                                        toward the sea

& you remind me, cap-haitian, of new orleans, nice
pointe-a-pitre, guadeloupe, with your old world feeling
wrought iron balconies holding voodoo loas
gods facing the sea, out beyond the harbor, crisscrossing tight
little narrow streets packed with black people squatting & fanning
themselves, like frogs in the claustrophobic heat, panting in rare shade
as red hot hibiscuses stick out their long tongues
like tongues of lovers searching for each others mouths
sweet, as in this sudden switch of breeze tonguing in now
from the atlantic, caresses the oldest black
capital of haiti, caresses me

& in another quick switch up, you are sweltering again
there on the bay, in may, cap-haitian, waiting for another cool
breeze to tongue in, gone away, now, like all the tourists gone
with all that money you need
                        the money your sweating people beg from me
right now, as eye speak through this poem
burning up inside the furnace of your noonday heat
you, cap haitian, spread out there
full of dazzling green carrying torches of flaming mimosas
& rainbow palettes of your famous, gingerbread houses

spread out, holding flowers, beautiful
as the faces of your people are beautiful
cap-haitian, bright with greetings & smiles

ancient black city, tucked into the elbow crook of the harbor
you climb your architecture slowly up the mountain

like an old man & woman climb stiff their creaking, stairs

In Jimmy's Garden
For James Baldwin (1924 — 1987)

this sunday morning breaks blue clear, in st paul de vence
the november dew glazing green grass, luminous, here where
the crowned soul of sunlight slants beamed glances of gold across
& over the gabled, slate, 300 year old rooftop of the gentle black
man, sleeping here, swallowed up by a mackintosh shirt, that is a tent
wrapped around his vanishing body, his mind still alert & beautiful
as this bird, singing valley, in southern france
where eye hear, now, a dog barking deep in the muffled distance
where tire wheels spin & wear their licking, rubber speech,mimicking
wind voices spinning themselves, in a constant rush, over asphalt,
brush my ears here, like gushing sounds of sea & sand ground up
into crushed dreams, whispering for the listener

& here & now & under this canopied trellis of grape leaves
in summer gone frost brown & yellow now with coming winter
eye focus my poet's camera, through this pen eye am using now
& see these hills, wrapping themselves, like legs of a sensuous
woman around this poem, like similar valleys & mountains in haiti
& so eye transport myself here & now over 5000 miles to that place
tortured with hunger, sudden death, voodoo & wafting smoke
curling up sea-green valleys — like here — stinging nostrils
& ask for the hougon's help in delivering this deep sleeping
wordsmith, shrinking up under the slate, gabled roof
chewing, invisible, piranha teeth, tearing away his flesh

& here & now, in this early breaking, sun-blue, moment, he is
moving pass it all, in deep knowing, to a peaceful place
beyond this sweet adopted space of torture miraculous with glory
the poetry of birds & sea sound of wheels fusing their speech
mimicking wind voices licking rubber over asphalt

& he is moving beyond all of us, now, even his brother's voice
breaking low in his bedroom mingling with a former lover's murmur
raising in the 300 year old farmhouse, like the new coffee brewing
in the pot, in this new day & we will be warmed by the croissants
heating in the ancient oven, where the old smiling french woman
is bent over, now, while above my aging head
brown shrivelled grapes, die on the vine —
prisoners of time & fate — like you
O great wordsmith — "mouth on paper of the revolution" —
your spirit, now, moving beyond even the wings of night

your spirit, now, moving & fusing, with the light

In Memoriam
For James Baldwin (1924 - 1987)

it's like a gray, dreary day, wet with tears & mourning
when someone you love ups & goes away
leaving behind a hole in your laughter, an empty space
following you around, like an echo you always hear & never see
high up in the mountains
the spirit gone & left, circling, there, its diminishing sound
a song looking for a place inside this gray day of tears
to lay down its earthly load
to drop down its weary voice among the many blue ones missing
there, who are elbowing their clacking bones, rattling, like false teeth
loose in a jelly jar, up against each other, their voices
dead as lead, & silence yawning
with the indifference final breaths acheive
& the open mouths are black holes framing endless space
words fall through, like stars sprinkled through the breath
of your holy sentences, jimmy
up there now with the glorious voice of bessie
the glory hallelujah, shouting gospel
you loved so deeply, wrote it out in your blood
running like dazzling rivers of volcanic lava, blood
so dazzling, your words blooming van gogh sunflowers
you planted, as sacred breaths inside our minds & hearts
the image of the real deal going down funky & hard

& so we celebrate you, holy witness, celebrate
your skybreaking smile, infectuous laughter
hear your glory hallelujah warnings everywhere we look
see clearly, the all-american, scrubbed down, button down
greed, rampant, in these "yet to be united states"
& so we take heed, beg for your forgiveness, that you might
forgive us for our smallness, for not rising up with you

for being less than our awesome, pitiful needs
forgive us now in your silence, jimmy
forgive us all who knew & were silent & fearful
& forgive us all, O wordsaint, who never even listened
forgive us for all the torture, for all the pain

Avalanche Aftermath
For Earl Maxie

outside lake tahoe, we see, scorched, white bones
of stake-like trees, felled (& they remind of crude war
weapons, sharpened & hidden & pointing up from pits)
cutting a wide path through murmuring green
pines, pointing their branches, accusingly up, at a steel blue
spring sky, crystal clear above our voices, where the highway once
loped & looped back, winding down from echo summit
the year before half the mountain walked clean across the american river
intact, to the other side of the road, thrown there after an avalanche
triggered abrupt & permanent change in the way things were
like a track of train rails, switching up directions, after
the juice is thrown at the main, power station: & it reminds
us, destinations are always still in the hands of God

Porter, at 18 Months
For Porter Troupe

you slipped down into this world, porter
during the dead hours of night
slipped down in a form already pefect, kicking
a screaming bursting from your new, ballooning lungs
older than time, though young in this miraculous
moment of celebration
& you were the mysterious, meaning of magic, porter
the fused dialectic of passion, alchemized
a sweet miracle, beyond all words

& now, already, you speak in a strange tongue
to birds & ants
           & now, already, you terrorize the cat
from his sun-nap, & draw your exploding imagination
over all the clean walls
           & now, already, you reject
with disdain, all helping hands
& go about your business in your own way

full of wonder, we watch you grow into yourself
filling out your own imagination, charting your own course
like an explorer, discovering new worlds
opening up before you, like flowers

& we are both amazed & afraid, knowing the way
in front of you will be treacherously beautiful
having travelled this road, before

so now, we teach you bonding principles, absent of miracles
but soon — very soon — we will stand aside & let you go

Porter at Bailliff, Guadeloupe
For Porter Troupe

them flies attacked in bailliff, like angry bees
dive-bombing kamikazes, swarming all around our son
poor porter, swinging his arms, like skinny little wind mills
crying up a storm, spraying spit everwhichaway
outside in the sweet open air of la casa
restaurant, sprawled across wet rocks, hard by a soft blue caribbean sea
& me trying to explain to him them flies wouldn't bite him
all the while flailing my own arms like a mad karate man kung-fu-ing
gnats, trying too keep them off my own banana flambe
but porter wasn't having none of that sweet talk
eye was giving him, nor offers of sugar-coated, chocolate soldier candy
all he wanted to do was get on up & out of there
leave that wondrous view of shimmering
piano notes, skittering, like flashing, silver minnows skimming
the dazzling surface of salt water, behind him
leave it & get on down the road, where he could talk in the cool
height of mountains, look at the cows
& goats mowing down grassy knolls around him
& leave all them dive-bombing, kamikaze flies, behind
leave them & hold on tight to his now vexed soul

Change
For Margaret & Porter ▬▬▬▬▬▬▬▬▬▬▬▬▬▬▬▬▬▬▬▬▬▬▬▬▬▬▬▬▬▬▬▬▬▬

use to be eye would be laying there
in margaret's lap, longside her sweet
soft thighs, on sunday mornings, sipping
champagne, sucking on her soft, open lips
drinking in the love from her moist, brown eyes
now, porter's there, giggling, twenty month old
squirming squeals — a tiny, spitting image of me —
his eyes kissing everyone, including me, & me?
well, eye'm stting here, apart from them
hungry, alone, in my favorite chair
watching television
& watching them, watching me

Simple Joys

my young son, porter, watching snowflakes
whoops, in ecstasy, as they collect, like lint
on the front windshield of my car, his growing
hands try to snag them through the tinted glass
as they hit & melt, like dead faces time erases
in a flash, though he misses & leaves only his
handprints on the tinted glass, there, his sudden
simple joy of discovering, suddenly, switching
like the attention span of television
his eyes now locked onto spinning, car wheels
churning in surprise, his imagination scotchtaping
itself to everything, tripping over everything, turning
snowflakes into flowers, brown brushstrokes stroking
the windshield become the tail of our cat, tchikaya
window bars, baseball bats in the eyes of his dazzling
invention, wonder residing there, like magic
everyday the curtain going up on his transforming
pure eyes, that see metaphors everywhere
& it gives me sweet joy in this age of cynicism
to watch & be with him, tripping through discovery —
his simple joys the envy of my caged wisdom

Eye Walk

eye walk, liquid footsteps of my words
across tongue bridge, to where you stand
just now, offer you these bittersweet syllables
pregnant with history of what
we have seen together, metaphors,
as in the color of sea breezes & wind, rustling
hairdos of trees, tossing & turning in the ebb & flow
of meaning between us, the rhythms of your seduction
flowing into sound of your body breathing
just outside, now, my ears, where your licking
tongue — a breeze, blowing softly — teases
your voice, a mere whisper & your pouting lips
shaping a kiss, succulent, as a plum, bursting

Tout de Meme — Nice & Malibu

the cote d'azur
like the coast of malibu —
a necklace of lights

Influences
In memory of Romare Bearden

blue space between chords
        father hines scats piano
clues: romare's bold strokes

21 Lines To Carnot, Guadeloupian Master Drummer

his wood & zinc house hard by the bay in goyave
carnot, master of traditional, guadeloupian, le woz
drumming, six other palm to skin rhythms, he of the flying
hands, cracking thunder, he splits the silent speech of night
machete fingers cleaving a passageway
voices flowing through ancestral
cadences, pulsating lyrical, voodoo, sewing breezes
painting pastel music, from deep inside itself
a secret language swells the way to magic, ritual
whose ears have heard the mystery of love, unfolding

holding the history of doves, a sea crab scuttles over
the stone floor, cold & hard, as poverty, carnot leans, strong
his body, an exclamation mark —
& sharp as a honed, sword's blade, the edges torn & jagged
as starpoints screwed into his peasant, catfish eyes
the electric boring up deep simmering coals, burning from within
the steady gaze, hawk-like, holds the sky
cruising through his two, brown lagoons —
leans into the sea, salted wind, where he goes
a fisherman, drumming, his life, the last of his kind here —

african roots dropping secret notes from his palms

Poem For My Father
For Quincy T. Troupe Sr.

father, it was an honor to be there, in the dugout
with you, the glory of great black men swinging their lives
as bats, at tiny white balls
burning in at unbelievable speeds, riding up & in & out
a curve breaking down wicked, like a ball falling off a table
moving away, snaking down, screwing its stitched magic
into chitling circuit air, its comma seams spinning
toward breakdown, dipping, like a hipster
bebopping a knee-dip stride, in the charlie parker forties
wrist curling, like a swan's neck
behind a slick black back
cupping an invisible ball of dreams

& you there, father, regal, as an african, obeah man
sculpted out of wood, from a sacred tree, of no name, no place, origin
thick branches branching down, into cherokee & someplace else lost
way back in africa, the sap running dry
crossing from north carolina into georgia, inside grandmother mary's
womb, where your mother had you in the violence of that red soil
ink blotter news, gone now, into blood graves
of american blues, sponging rococo
truth long gone as dinosaurs
the agent-oranged landscape of former names
absent of african polysyllables, dry husk consonants there
now, in their place, names, flat, as polluted rivers
& that guitar string smile always snaking across
some virulent, american, redneck's face
scorching, like atomic heat, mushrooming over nagasaki
& hiroshima, the fever blistered shadows of it all
inked, as etchings, into sizzled concrete

but you, there, father, through it all, a yardbird solo
riffing on bat & ball glory, breaking down the fabricated myths
of white major league legends, of who was better than who
beating them at their own crap game, with killer bats,
as bud powell swung his silence into beauty of a josh
gibson home run, skittering across piano keys of bleachers
shattering all manufactured legends up there in lights
struck out white knights, on the risky edge of amazement
awe, the miraculous truth sluicing through
steeped & disguised in the blues
confluencing, like the point at the cross
when a fastball hides itself up in a slider, curve
breaking down & away in a wicked, sly grin
curved & posed as an ass-scratching uncle tom, who
like old sachel paige delivering his famed hesitation pitch
before coming back with a hard, high, fast one, is slicker
sliding, & quicker than a professional hitman —
the deadliness of it all, the sudden strike
like that of the "brown bomber's" crossing right
of sugar ray robinson's, lightning, cobra bite

& you, there, father, through it all, catching rhythms of chono
pozo balls, drumming, like conga beats into your catcher's mitt
hard & fast as "cool papa" bell jumping into bed
before the lights went out

of the old, negro baseball league, a promise, you were
father, a harbinger, of shock waves, soon come

Poem For the Root Doctor of Rock n Roll
For Chuck Berry

& it all came together on the mississippi river
chuck, you there riding the rocking-blue sound wave
duck-walking the poetry of hoodoo down
                  & you were the mojo-hand
of juju crowing, the gut-bucket news — running it down
for two records sold to make a penny
back then in those first days, "majoring in mouth" —
a long, gone, lean lightning rod
             picking the edge, charging the wires
                  of songs, huckle-bucking "roll over
beethoven", playing "devil's music", till white devils stole it from you
& called it their own, "rock n roll"
                devils like elvis & pat boone
who never duck-walked back in the alley with you
& bo diddley, little richard & the fatman from new orleans
all yall slapping down songs meaner than the smell
of toejam & rot-gut whiskey breath
back there, in them back rooms
            of throw down

back there, where your song lyrics grew, like fresh corn
you, chuck berry, an authentic american genius of barbecue sauce
& deep fried catfish licks, jack-salmon guitar
               honky-tonk rhythms
jangling warm, vibrating sounds, choo-chooing train
whistles fiddling & smoking down the tracks of the blues
motivating through "little queenie", "maybelline"
decked out in red on sarah & finney
alarms rolling off your whipping tongue
in the words of "johnny b good"

you clued us in, back to the magical hookup of ancestors
their seamless souls threading your breath
                                    their blood in your sluicing strut
& to much "monkey business", the reason for their deaths, cold & searing
your spirit reaching down to the bones of your roots
deep in the "show me" blood of missouri soil
                                    your pruned, hawk-look, profiling
where you rode your white cadillac of words, cruising
the highways of language (what we speak & hear even now)
breathing inside your cadences
                            you shaped & wheeled the music
duck-walking the length of the stage
duck-walked your zinging metaphors of everyday
slip-slide & strut, vibrating your hummingbird wings
your strumming style, the cutting edge
& you were what was to come

so hail, hail, chuck berry, root doctor of "rock n roll"
authentic american genius
                            tonguing deep in river syllables
hail, hail, chuck berry, laying down the motivating juju
you great, american, mojo hand

root doctor, spirit, of american, "rock n roll"

166

They Say the Hoochiecoochie Man Done up an Gone
For Troy Porter, "the boss in the hot sauce"

you were the heart-healing, glory, back then, when you sang
your fat-back, collard green, doodoo, blood flames, choochooing
train whistles, that broke double string guitars, washboarding gin
scrapings & funky-butt, sapphire-stars — jewelled fingers hip on hips —
these mojo, double-clutchings, were your calling cards, juju
pain framing your call & response, muddy river, hot sauce, you
"boss in the hot sauce", like troy, add catfish & no-count cracker bosses
mean up in your voice, speaking of no nonsense
now, they tell me your white lightning, hoodoo, done up an gone
done went an stuck in your throat, like a needle, or like a chicken bone
caught in the tangled words of some sinning preacher
that's what they tell me, old sweet, hot sauce, that's what they say
that your deep, secret, healing song, done gone & catch there
in the web of drink & dope, like dew do to moss in the early morning
glory & your song is now caught there in a death choice of pure-de-
constipation, boy, that's what they tell me, son, that's what they saying
now, boy, that silence is boss of your juke-joint hoodoo
tell me that your voodoo done sunk, pitiful, as rivers running low
O blood deep, delta soothsayer, whose songs once echoed bones
running & weeping beneath the mississippi's unmarked graves
were the tombstones, marking those spirits, who laid down heavy loads
so tell me, "boss in the hot sause", where all the magic done gone, now
gone out your double-edged songs, your guitar choking, boss baritone
of the rusty-razored voice of to much gin & whiskey
rot gut dues, utterance, of blue magic, hoodoo, buried deep
in your hot sauce, boss, so where the hoochiechoochie, sawblading
blues lyrics done took themselves, brother, vowel-stretching
voice selling wolf-tickets, calling moonbreaks down
they tell me your two-timing songs, knee-deep in history
done up & gone silent now, forever clued into your bloodshot voice

eyes imitating two blown out lightbulbs, baby, they say
your double clutching blues done gone the way of deaf-mutes
that's what they say, blood brother of the hard, cold way
hoochiechoochie flame-thrower, that's what they all say

Reflections On Growing Older

eye sit here, now, inside my fast thickening breath
the whites of my catfish eyes, muddy with drink
my roped, rasta hair snaking down in twisted salt & pepper
vines braided from the march of years, pen & ink lines etching
my swollen face, the collected weight of years swelling
around my middle, the fear of it all overloading circuits
here & now with the weariness of tears, coming on in storms
the bounce drained out of my once liquid strut
a stork-like gimpiness there now, stiff as death
my legs climbing steep stairs in protest now, the power gone
slack from when eye once heliocoptered through cheers,
    hung around rims
threaded rainbowing jumpshots, that ripped, popped cords
    & envious peers
gone, now the cockiness of that young, firm flesh
perfect as arrogance & the belief that perpetual hard-ons would
    swell forever here,
smoldering fire in a gristle's desire, drooping limp now
like wet spaghetti, or noodles, the hammer-head that once shot
straight in ramrod hard into the sucking sweet heat
    of wondrous women
wears a lugubrious melancholy now, like an old frog wears
    its knobby head
croaking like a lonely malcontent through midnight hours
& so eye sit here, now, inside my own gathering flesh
thickening into an image of humpty-dumpty
at the edge of a fall, the white of my hubris gone
muddy as mississippi river water
eye feel now the assault of shotgunned years
shortening breath, charlie horses throbbing through cold
tired muscles, slack & loose as frayed, old ropes

slipping from round the neck of an executed memory
see, now, these signals of irreversible breakdowns —
the ruination of my once, perfect flesh — as medals earned
fighting through the holy wars of passage, see them as miracles
of the glory of living breath, pulsating music through my poetry - -
syncopating metaphors turned here inside out - -
see it all now as the paths taken, the choices made
the loves lost & broken, the loves retained
& the poems lost & found in the dark
beating like drumbeats through the heart

Falling Down Roads of Sleep

we are falling down roads into sleep
falling into sleep from blues
posing as the sky, the eye of the Creator, moves
black cataracts of clouds around, pointillistic, as clues
wet, as when a bad knee tells us that rain is coming
before night floods down the streets
sleep is seducing, as the light
slips from the night, slips from our eyes
& slides across the sky, like feet over ice
the lances of our intentions, glancing off moons
slicing the edge of noon
we remember a sky blue & deep with light
remember the wings of birds turning around hours
burning off suns, flights of music diving toward night
like warring elements, our speech thunderclapping
down streets lugubrious with sleep
deep down we leap, back into sleep, so steep
the fall back into blues
we forget the fading of night, coming
begin climbing up ladders of song, rung by rung
sleep falling between our language, now, lifting
toward flight, rain clouds, like circling crows
cruise under light, under the bold
gold polished coin of the sun, holding

Untitled

in brussels, eye sat in the grand place cafe & heard
duke's place, played after salsa
between the old majestic architecture, jazz bouncing off
all that gilded gold history snoring complacently there
flowers all over the ground, up inside the sound
the old white band jammin the music
tight & heavy, like some food
pushin pedal to the metal
gettin all the way down
under the scaffolding surrounding
l'hotel de ville, chattanooga choochoo
choo chooing all the way home, upside walls, under gold eagles
& a gold vaulting girl, naked on a rooftop holding a flag over
her head, like skip rope, surrounded by all manner
of saints & gold madmen, riding emblazoned stallions
snorting like crazed demons at their nostrils
the music swirling like a dancing bear around
a beautiful girl, flowers all up in her hair

the air woven with lilting voices in this grand place of parapets
& crowns, jewels & golden torches streaming
like a horse's mane, antiquity riding through in a carriage wheel
here, through gargoyles & gothic towers rocketing swordfish
lanced crosses
pointing up at a God threatening rain
& it is stunning at this moment when raised beer steins cheer
the music on, hot & heavy, still humming & cooking
basic bebopping black rhythms alive here
in this ancient grand place of europe
this confluence point of nations & cultures
jumping off place for beer & cuisines

fused with music, poetry & stone
here in this blinding, beautiful square
sunlit now as the golden eye of God shoots through
flowers all over the cobbled ground, up in the music
the air brightly cool as light after jeweled rain

Following The North Star Boogaloo
For Miguel Algarin

following the north star boogaloo
the rhythm takes me
back to where music began
to percolate language like coffee in another form
back before frederick douglass laid it down
heavy on abe lincoln
when music was breakdancing, old hottentots
throwing down mean as bojangles ever did
now jump forward through history's dice game
pick up the steps of james brown
michael jackson moonwalking
the old blues talking about yo mama
now fast forward down the lane
pick up the dance of 5 brothers
skateboardin the court
out in the open, one closes the break
after taking it to the hole off the coast to coast
doing a 180 degree phi slamma jamma dunk
before they all high five & glad hand after
stamping their footprints all up in the paint
up in this poet's word dribble
a drummer's paradiddle
word up, yo bro, hip hop, rappers
skateboarding the go go out in the open
court of macking the holy ghost down

hey you, diddle-diddle, voodoo griot, take me
back to when eye was black & hittin proud
out on the slick bop thoroughfares
back before the mean homeboys rolled snarling
duckwaddle down the middle, eyes empty with death

174

before the alley-oops wore their lives as chips on shoulders
in stratuspheric attitudes, hung dip from wall to wall
chained gold, cap bills on heads quakin sideways
muscling up bold masterblasters
checking out reeboks
chillin dead up in the cut "fresh" as "death"
after "mo money", "mo money", "mo money"
check it out bro, pharmaceutical wizards
making 7 figure bank accounts do somersaults, it's no sweat
it's rolling in so fast for crack ("& it ain't nothing
but a hole in the wall") for homeboys
cash n carry, cold 16 year old's
who cant count nothing but greenbacks
sliding off the screen & roll, they heliocopter
after dipping & rolling down the middle
high up above the paint, their footprints walking on space
up over your face hang gliding to the basket, like praying mantis'
so fresh they make pootbutts faint slamming
faster than high fiving glory —
180 degrees of schoolboy legends, saints
unfolding in prime time memory

so roll it back, kojak, before magic's knees go permanently
south for the winter, & leave air jordan's footprints
in yo face game as the baddest one in town
before they change up the shake & bake, jam off the sky again with a new
phenom double clutching up there in space, like a ferrari stretching out
flat out burning up german autobahns, changing up the guard quicker
than fear brings down doodoo
but hey, young bro, flash the dice roll back through shit
to when the big O was jackknifing through all them bodies

out on the court, too when goose tatum was shimmying magic
down in the middle, down in the paint
as roy haynes jitterbugged like a magician
hoola hoopin' the ball around him, before fast forwarding to dr. j
     — Julius Erving!
& did we ever think we'd lose these hoodoo gods
to old age homes for roundball royalty
new age homeboys not even knowing who they are
& do they even know about jonestown, all them
bloated bodies cracking beneath the sun
& did they ever hear about the north carolina astronaut,
david skywalking thompson
jamming out in the open, off the fly
heliocoptering to roundball heaven
off the motherfucking coast to coast
before he took the fall for all that shit
he snorted up his nose, before hitting the pipe
that took him right on out like a blown lightbulb —
way back before kenny anderson was even
a glint in his parents pick n roll eyes

before he skateboarded off the juju fake
picked up his dribble, like magic
then rose up in space like hallelujah 4th of july
glory, before dropping a deuce or a trey quick
as a pickpocket off the slide by
sleight of hand trick, eased on by like mojo with his yoyo
pitter patter, now you see me, now you don't, yo bro
whodunit, poor guy got caught in kenny's schoolyard
voodoo, jump back in the alley
say what? did you see that motherfuckin bad-boy sky?
past where it all started, somewhee back before

language followed the north star boogaloo
dancing back when they was hamboning the black
bottom for fun, back then in the language
when homeboys picked cotton
played the dozens; "eye hate to talk about yo mama
she was a good old soul, but she got a two-ton pussy
& an iron ass hole, & yo daddy got a dick
big as a motherfucking toothpick!"

say what chu say, say what chu say? say what?

word, when we knew ourselves through songs
through what we saw alive in homeboys eyes
through love, through what it was we were before
commercials told us how to move & groove, who to love
when we did it all & had fun & knew the heros
new & old & never confused dope for the bomb
back before we fast forwarded to integration
entered the 60's on a bullshit tip
lost ourselves in the fast forwarding
70's & 80's, in the cloning xerox machines
before kenny anderson skateboarded
his prince of a hip hop, roundball game
breakrapping all the way to roundball legend

up north, south of the voodoo connection
north of where we entered from africa